Wh[illegible] Mitchell?

About the Author

Stephen Yeo taught History at Sussex University for many years before becoming Principal of Ruskin College in 1989. He has written about the history of voluntary associations of many kinds, including those connected to the Labour Movement. He sees adult education as part of that history. He is also interested in working-class writing and its organisations, helping to found QueenSpark Books and the Federation of Worker Writers and Community Publishers. He sees his current work on the interface between education and business as a Board Member of the Heart of England Training and Enterprise Council as one way in which he can try to keep faith with J.T.W. Mitchell.

WHO WAS J.T.W. MITCHELL?

by
Stephen Yeo

CWS Membership Services

Published by CWS Membership Services,
New Century House, Manchester M60 4ES

First published February 1995

British Library Cataloguing in Publication Data.
A catalogue record for this book is available from the British Library.

ISBN 0 85195 221 6

Designed and typeset by
CWS Membership Services

Printed in Great Britain by
The Co-operative Press Limited,
Progress House, Chester Road,
Manchester M16 9HP

PREFACE

This essay on J.T.W. Mitchell forms part of an ongoing project on the history of Co-operative and other forms of nineteenth and twentieth century working-class associations such as friendly societies, clubs and building societies. The essay outgrew the book for which it was intended, *New Views of Co-operation,* ed. Stephen Yeo (Routledge 1988) which contains a great deal of related material. Readers might also be interested in working class association, private capital, welfare and the state in the late-nineteenth and twentieth centuries in *Social Work ,Welfare and the State*, ed. Noel Parry, Michael Rustin and Carole Satyamurti (Arnold, 1979)

I would like to thank Graham Melmoth, Secretary of the CWS for his continued interest and Mervyn Wilson, Officer for Member Education of the Co-operative Union for helping to keep the Movement's enthusiasm for its own history alive and practical. Paddy Maguire, Andy Durr, Gill Scott and Peter Gurney have also talked with me about Mitchell and the Movement for many hours. Roy Garrett, the most genial of Librarians who died last year, disagreed with me over many cups of tea and pints of Guiness in Manchester. Many thanks also to Ursula Howard who helped me to turn a penultimate draft into (I hope) an intelligible essay worthy of its subject

Stephen Yeo
Ruskin College
Oxford
January 1995

Introduction by Graham Melmoth CWS Secretary

J.T.W. MITCHELL
A FOREWORD

The Sixteenth of March, 1995 sees the centenary of the death of J.T.W. Mitchell - the great President of the CWS. In this monograph, modestly described here as an essay, Stephen Yeo brings Mitchell vividly to life in a way that escaped the few who have so far attempted it, including William Maxwell, Mitchell's Scottish counterpart and friend, and the CWS Historian, Percy Redfern.

All that a later CWS chronicler, William Richardson, managed to say about Mitchell in a brief reference to him in his "CWS in War and Peace" (published by the CWS in 1977) was that "he did not intellectually evolve a case for the superiority of consumer over producer co-operation". Not only does this seem to miss the point but it captures the authentic flavour of the faint praise which Stephen Yeo suggests has damned Mitchell on all sides and which the author frequently encountered in his biographical quest. He argues convincingly that Mitchell was a radical thinker with a vision and a federalist project planted firmly in his working class roots. His adversaries, on the other hand, the idealists, who have had much the better of the press since Mitchell's death, were for the most part drawn from the gentler echelons of society and, as Stephen Yeo suggests, were uncomfortable with the idea that working men and women should be capable, unaided, of driving their own economic destiny.

The principal debt we owe Stephen Yeo in this work is the painstaking uncovering of Mitchell's credo from under a century of unflattering varnish. But we have him to thank too for catching the dynamism and the spirit of a man who for twenty years presided over one of the world's biggest businesses and yet who died with no family to mourn him, with few wordly possessions, whilst registering hardly a footnote in history. Here is an historian redressing the balance. 1995 is certainly the year to do it.

Graham Melmoth
January 1995

J. T. W. Mitchell,
Chairman of the C.W.S. from 1874 to 1895.

WHO WAS J.T.W. MITCHELL?

for H.E.Y. 1894 - 1957

I

To the extent that they can be discovered, I find the personal details strangely compelling. I will relate some of them here. But, to get to my main answer straight away, J.T.W. (John) Mitchell (1828-1895) - 'Mitchell, as he was familiarly called and will ever best be known' - (1) is an outstanding figure in the history of the nineteenth and twentieth-century working-class project. (2)

The most important fact about Mitchell is that he was Chairman of the Co-operative Wholesale Society from 1878 to 1895, re-elected Quarter by Quarter all through that period. By the late-1880's the turnover of the CWS exceeded £6m a year, its 'warehouse at Manchester is a small town', and it was administering nearly a £million of funds, in shares, loan capital and reserves. By 1897, there were 8,407 people employed by the Society, working in the distributive departments and in the bank, as well as in the productive works and services. (3)

So who was Mitchell? I shall argue that he was, in essence, a late nineteenth century Owenite, with strong early nineteenth century plebeian-radical connections. By this I mean he believed in singular, complete solutions to society's problems. He did not call himself a socialist, though the word 'socialistic' was applied to his enterprise. (4) While acknowledging Robert Owen as, 'if not the actual founder of associated effort as understood today, at least the inspirer of the thoughts and aims of those who at one period or another have become the leaders of the Co-operative Movement', Mitchell knew his history and, therefore, had his doubts. 'So far as I can gather, he did not believe so much in co-operation; he thought the tribe of merchants could do business for them as well as they could do it for themselves'. 'Choosing to do their own business instead of allowing other people to do it for them' was one of Mitchell's favourite ways of describing his project. It sounded innocent, part of an Englishman's birthright. But he knew how radical a project it was, and how many vested interests it was already disturbing. (5) Mitchell's most famous maxim: Never despise the store! was a rebuke to Robert Owen who, of course, did just that. (6)

Mitchell was a thinker. But he was wary of 'theory' and 'theorists'. In terms of conventional nineteenth century political categories, he was a Radical or Advanced Liberal. He very occasionally referred to himself as a 'collectivist', but this was not a favoured label and 'not', he pointed out in 1894, 'not by Act of Parliament'. (7) He was certainly strongly anti-individualist, even anti-individual, espousing only 'an individuality for the good of all'. 'Co-operation ought to be based on the principle of united interest with the societies and not individuals. Some persons taught that the individual should be the basis'. (8) Mitchell's was a quite specifically un-bourgeois life, making it ironic (no, offensive) that he and his movement have been used so much by labour historians as indices of the embourgeoisement of the working class. Full of talent which Beatrice Webb, for one, saw as business genius, Mitchell's was not an ordinary 'career'. It remains an extraordinary fact about the man, the movement, and the peculiarities of the English that the Chairman of 'the most varied if not the largest business enterprise in the world at that time' received something like £150 a year in fees and died worth £350/17s/8d. (9) And this at a time when (to use a Mitchell phrase) in 'the Barnum wickedness of the competitive world' (10), conspicuous consumption by capitalists, on the one hand and self-regarding professional management as a separate social group (class?) on the other, were busy establishing themselves. 'Perhaps no man in Europe presided over so large a business, and certainly no man ever presided over so vast a concern who took such slender remuneration for so doing' (11). The bedroom in which he died in John Street, Rochdale was 'humble in the extreme'. It contained some of the old furniture his mother had when he was a boy, 'reports and balance sheets.....took the place of ordinary literature' - though Mitchell liked books - and there were portraits of a few friends, his Bible and hymn book, and 'that was all'. (12)

II

Mitchell's funeral in Rochdale on Wednesday, March 20th 1895 was a very public affair. (13)

It was conducted by the Co-operative Wholesale Society, 'the deceased gentleman having no near relatives upon whom the duty could be supposed to fall'. Very few among the many wreaths at Milton Congregational Chapel, where Mitchell had been a Deacon, bore the names of individuals. It was not as though he did not love and was not loved. 'He stood that truest of all tests, that of closest intimacy and companionship. Our departed friend at least was not like the stage-trappings of the theatre, best seen at a distance; on the other hand, the nearer you got to him the more you liked him and the more thoroughly you understood the man and appreciated the all-pervading motives of his life'. (14) One of the two people in the world closest to him was Abraham Howard, 'his close friend till his dying day'. 'They were like Damon and Phintias - their mutual confidence and esteem being only equalled by the strength of their attachment'. (15) The other very close friend was Thomas Butterworth. (16) At one time, Butterworth had been in disgrace in Rochdale: in prison, for stealing from a Co-op. When he was released in about 1872, Mitchell held out his hand in friendship. They became inseparable. Butterworth inherited some property, 'yet because of Mitchell's kindness be became his willing serving man'. He lived nearby and would send his servant in to clean for Mitchell and himself ran messages, packed suitcases and so on, 'the neighbours frequently remarking that if Mr. Mitchell died, Mr. Butterworth would have to accompany him, as he could not exist alone'. In the event, they died within a few days of each other, Butterworth not lasting long enough even to attend Mitchell's funeral.

So the first carriage in the procession to Rochdale Cemetery, in late March 1895, contained Mr. Meather, Butterworth's executor - Butterworth was to have been Mitchell's - and 'some who had been near to him in his domestic life': Miss Wilby of Ossett, Yorks, and Miss Miller. This was followed by a carriage containing four cousins. And they were the only private mourners, in a procession which stretched without a break from Milton, down Smith Street, over Wellington Bridge and along South Parade to a point opposite the magnificent Town Hall, arguably itself a civic response to Co-operation. Within Milton Chapel 'perfect order and decency' prevailed, 'the greatest order was maintained throughout'. Careful arrangements had been made and 'these were strictly adhered to'. (17) The Minister and six Deacons entered at exactly one o'clock. One pew immediately behind the clock in the south galley remained unoccupied, 'heavy black drapings marked it out as the place of him who will sit there no more'. The body of the Chapel was reserved for delegates from Co-operative Societies, the space at the rear under the gallery for representatives of local bodies (I take this distinction between delegates and representatives direct from the local press), the aisle to the right of the entrance was for teachers and scholars at the Sunday School where Mitchell had been active from scholar to superintendent for fifty years, week in and week out. The aisle to the left was kept for members of Milton congregation .

The night before, the coffin had been taken from number 15 John Street, 'a dark and sullen abode'. Mitchell had never lived more than a few hundred yards from there, though in five or six different rooms or houses. For more than twenty years, he lived absolutely by himself.

The Sunday School movement had been his break. 'But for the help of the Sunday School, it is doubtful whether we should have known anything about him'. (18) He would not talk about the circumstances of his birth even with close friends. At his funeral the Minister said that in his prayers at Sunday School 'the word "Father" seemed ever on his lips' and that he, Mitchell, was a father to the school with 'forbearance carried almost to a fault, if he had a fault in School work'. (19)

He was the illegitimate son of 'a man in good position but of ungoverned character'. (20) 'His forefathers (had) for generations been engaged in hat manufacture', a trade which became extinct in Rochdale during the early 1850's. (21) His mother was poor. She kept him out of the factories for as long as she could, until he was 10 or 11 when he went to work as a piecer for 18 pence a week. Other children started at 7 or 8. Relating this experience to profit-sharing versions of co-operation later on, Mitchell said: 'Whatever profit might have been handed to me I do not see that I could have done more'. (22) His mother kept John and herself partly by taking lodgers, partly by running a beerhouse. She sent him to learn reading and writing at a school in Bailie Street. This was on Sundays and was run by a clerk in a foundry. Then John moved to another Sunday class.

One day in 1846 two men (one of whom was at his funeral in 1895) were canvassing the streets around Hope Street for the Providence Chapel Sunday School. In the Mitchell house they found the boy reading and his mother making the dinner. 'They seemed to live on the most affectionate terms'. They asked John to join. His mother agreed. The next Sunday one of the men, Mr. Pagan, called for him and joined Mitchell to his own class.

> 'Here Mitchell for the first time in his life discovered that he really had no opinions, either religious or political. A new life seemed to burst upon him... Up to that time he said his mother had been his only friend.' (23)

Signing the pledge must have been a big decision: it meant breaking with one of his mother's only visible means of support.

Associational life in one of the largest of all nineteenth century voluntary associations, Sunday Schools, was now added to Mitchell's daily working hours which were from 6 in the morning until 7.30 at night. He used the library at Providence Sunday School. He joined their Juvenile Temperance Society, which led him into the Rochdale Temperance Society, of which he became a committee member. He also became a member of the local Rechabite tent which became the 'Love and Truth' division of the Sons of Temperance. He remained a member and official until he died. The sub-committee of the Temperance Society held meetings in Mitchell's room at the top of his mother's house. Then, in about 1850, Mitchell personally experienced secession - a characteristic event in the associational culture of the day. There was disagreement at Providence about the appointment of a new pastor. A number of members split to form the new Milton Congregational Church in Bailie Street. Mitchell went with them. By 1854 he was a Milton Sunday School teacher.

Mr. Pagan did more than recruit and teach his young client. He owned a flannel mill and offered Mitchell a situation in the warehouse at 16/- a week. The firm changed hands several times. Mitchell stayed for eighteen years, until 1867, and was promoted from wool sorter to manager of the wool department. In the Minute Books of the General Committee of Rochdale Equitable Pioneers Society in May 1868, he referred to himself as 'Manager' of John Street. By June 1871, he was 'Manufacturer', having set himself up in trade as a flannel dealer. He did this on his own account for some years until he gradually let it go, as his work in the Co-operative Movement became too demanding.

Mitchell was clearly a man who itched for organisational work and the chance to do business. This was his life-time affair. His contacts in the flannel trade later led to his appointment as liquidator of the Lancashire and Yorkshire Productive

Society, a co-operative concern at Littleborough which hit bad times. From 1878 until the end of his life, he nursed that company round, contributing to attacks on his probity, to which I shall return. No one else had hope for the Society. But for much of his working life, even while at the CWS, Mitchell worked everyday between 7.30 and 9.30 in the morning to try to make it viable. Finally, he managed to free it from creditors and prepare it for takeover by the CWS. Mitchell had established a London agency to run his own business, getting cotton goods made by the Rochdale Manufacturing Society dyed and finished at Middleton which he then sold through this agency. He used his home as a warehouse, adding an adjoining cottage as the business grew. It is not clear exactly what the relations were between Mitchell's private trading at this time and the local societies with which he was connected. When his London agent failed, it was a blow, for Mitchell had held him in high regard. 'From this time he allowed his business quietly to slip away from him as he was giving all his time and attention to the Wholesale business'. (24) There is no doubt that the man, later to be nicknamed 'Baron Wholesale' (25), had it in him to become boss of a very different kind of business empire.

III

However, he did not. He added Rochdale Co-operation to his Sunday School, Congregational, Temperance and other reforming associations. He joined the Pioneers in 1853. Through the Rochdale Equitable Pioneers Society, he was elected to the Board of the Co-operative Wholesale Society in 1869 and, in June 1874, became its Chairman. He held this position for the rest of his life. I will return to the details of his Rochdale Co-operative work, which are key elements in understanding what an associationist life, for labour, meant.

But first I am going to step aside from his story to look at it in the light of other people's views: that somewhat dim light in which Mitchell has been bathed ever since his death. For Mitchell himself wrote practically nothing. There are his public speeches and activity, at Congress for instance - though it is interesting that he wrote no papers for Congress in all the years of his attendance from 1869 - 95. Nor did he write articles in the CWS *Annuals* which were such an emblem of the Movement, often given as gifts of honour. We can watch him at work in his most characteristic setting, at the Quarterly Meetings of the CWS and its various committees, recorded in the Minutes or in the *Co-operative News*: or listen to him at the endless foundation stone ceremonies, tea parties, industrial exhibitions, etc. which he attended for local Co-operative Societies. From such material, it is possible to piece together his ideas, though less easy to trace where they came from. I will attempt to do this in subsequent sections of this essay.

Mitchell has been subject to an immense weight of opinion about him, however, as well as all this public material. His is not a name widely known outside the Co-operative Movement. Within the Movement, his after-life - his historical aura - has not been positive. Damnation and faint praise slipped out of the sides of the mouths of many people in the Movement, as I went about my research. It was like a lingering smell. This was coupled with incredulity that I should be interested in finding out about Mitchell at all. We all seem to know what he was about: namely taking co-operation ('idealism') out of the Co-op, and lining his own pocket, or maybe just his stomach, in the process.

The history of the Co-operative Movement during the second half of the nineteenth century (climaxing in the 1880's) has commonly been seen as a contest between goodies and baddies. The goodies were 'idealists', Christian Socialists, believers in producer co-operation. The baddies were materialists, shopkeepers, working men around the Co-operative Wholesale Society, believers in 'consumers co-operation'. Arguments between them centred on the rights of workers within producer co-ops. These rights were to shared control. They were also economic, variously called the 'bonus to labour', 'co-partnership', 'profit-sharing'. Mitchell was against such economic rights, in so far as they were to be realised at the points of production, i.e. at the level of the firm rather than at the level of the Co-operative, or wider society. He was, it is commonly suggested, on the wrong side and worse; on the big side: and it won. By the early twentieth century, the CWS position had, broadly speaking, won out within the mainstream Co-operative Movement. Mitchell, therefore, so that story has gone, was party to - and symbolic of - the long corruption of the co-operative ideal in the hands of the working class Co-operative Movement. This has been summed up by historians as 'from community building to shopkeeping': a long descent from Owenism. (26)

Yet perhaps this historical inheritance carefully unravelled can tell us about more than Mitchell.

Inside his own Movement and during his own life time, there was smoke which I find more interesting than the small fires behind it. Immediately after his death, there were difficulties surrounding some of his private or public effects, following the death of his beloved executor, Butterworth. The problem, as it appears in the General Committee Minutes of the CWS, was to get insignia -silver trowels, medals, a silver watch and a gold one too - out of Mitchell's house and into CWS keeping. There does seem to have been some aggravation about this. (27) What is interesting about it, perhaps - and very much in line with the feel of his funeral - is that the Society had no hesitation in regarding gifts made to Mitchell as their own rather than private to him and his heirs. Who was J.T.W. Mitchell? Answer: Chairman of the Co-operative Wholesale Society. More than Chairman: the CWS incarnate (28) or - this was a very common epithet - its spouse, or father: and was there ever a more loving husband or father that ever looked after his progeny better? (29) The relationship undoubtedly involved a particular quality of commitment. People wanted to understand it. It is interesting that the metaphor most available derived from marriage. The fact that Mitchell appeared to live happily alone was a puzzle too.

As the Minister of Milton Chapel said at his funeral:

> 'In the days of his fatal illness, it did seem a little sad that in a domestic sense he was so lonely. Doubtless family ties would have cheered and enriched his life. But no one was more bright and cheery than he.' (30)

As I hope to show, people have had category problems with Mitchell. Why, after all, make him married - assimilating him to familial forms which involve commitment, for sure, but of a different order to Mitchell's public work - when he had no wife, no daughter or son, no known father, and when he spent his spirit trying to include the whole world rather than a single partner, whether for business or emotional support, in his

Society? It is as if the only way to offer themselves explanation and consolation for Mitchell's apparently happy and fulfilled temperament in such an odd life was to invent a married state for him, to contain him in a framework of social normality - to bring him in from the margins and cut him down to size. For the family metaphor does serve as a subtraction, from an inclusive enterprise which was (still is) unfamiliar, not least in its degree of commitment to giant working class enterprise and in its creativity about non-bourgeois forms of association. Whatever else the Co-operative Wholesale Society was, it was not a typical late nineteenth century private firm. (31)

Why, too, make him corrupt - that lingering smell - unless that is the only available way of understanding (and subtracting from) a large, dynamic association *different* from the dominant, bourgeois ones around it, with different ambition, different ways of working, a different 'ethic'?

Allegations of corruption have been crude - financial corruption: 'he's only in it for the money' - and the corruption of ideals. Even though the smoke has not drifted far enough outside the Movement for many people to be aware of it, it may be worth looking directly into the fire. A dozen years before his death, there had been disquiet, some of it directed specifically at Mitchell, over 'fees and fares' paid to CWS directors. This turned into 'agitation' in the early summer of 1884. (32) Mitchell was on a delegation to the United States at the time. His co-directors became anxious when the delegation came back later than anticipated. They were in trouble.

To the 1990's eye, accustomed to private excess, the amounts spent on directors' expenses seem modest. It is the disquiet about them rather than their amounts which is most revealing. It is evidence of a belief in equality, healthy Jacobinism which can be picked up almost anywhere in the nineteenth and early twentieth century socialist and labour movement press and which still exists today, for instance in C.I.U. clubs. Money is bound to be a problem for working class, democratic associations in capitalism. When who gets it and how they get it are not noticed, democratic forms decay, or become purely commercial. Matters of principle are involved. If money matters are not seen as matters of principle, working class organisations inevitably degenerate.

Details are important. The form of payment for Directors of the CWS during the late 1870's was a fee of 2/6d per meeting. (33) There was also a per diem fee of 12/- for work away from Manchester, for example visiting Ipswich or the U.S.A. (34) When Mitchell attended the laying of a foundation stone for the Ipswich Society, he was away two nights and was paid 36/-, this transaction being a distinct item of business passing through a General Committee meeting - in effect the Board of one of the largest companies in the world - on January 23rd 1885. The local Society would probably also have offered him something, 'just such an acknowledgment as they chose to give. Be it ever so small, there was never a murmur as to its inadequacy for the service, even when it was barely sufficient to cover his travelling expenses, and not always even that' (35). The total spent on directors' expenses in 1883 was £3,800. In 1879, the CWS was spending 4d. in the £ on management costs. This amounted to 1.75% in a trading concern with a capital of £400,000 and with £600,000 worth of annual business. 'He (Mitchell) did not think there was a business of the same magnitude in the Kingdom that was managed so economically'. (36)

The important things within the Movement, however, were the forms of accountability. The fees and fares issue came up in part because it was felt during 1885 that the General Committee had exceeded their powers in passing a resolution on December 30th 1884 in which they had authorised the payment of fares on the same basis as in 1874, without calling a General Meeting. At a Quarterly Meeting in September 1879, the delegate from Eccles asked whether it had been necessary for the whole

General Committee to travel up to London for the laying of the foundation stone of the new CWS building in Leman Street. This was a good question: trips to London are at a premium, still, in movements among less well-off people. Chairman Mitchell took the point but said yes, in his judgment it was necessary, in order to demonstrate the success of 'true co-operation' in a city in which the Co-op had long had difficulty and in which spurious 'civil service' forms of co-operative trading had a head start. Visibility was advisable, he thought, particularly in a year in which a Select Committee was investigating these other forms of ersatz co-operation. These were widely-aired matters, in meetings and in elaborate press reports. When asked in 1881 why the cost of reporting meetings in the *Co-operative News* had increased dramatically, Mitchell replied that the Committee had been accused of concealment because of the brevity of earlier reports. So now they employed Henry Pitman, formerly editor of *The Co-operator*, and carried five page reports of their meetings in a form of public Minutes. We are dealing with a world business, which, when Mitchell was on his deathbed, sent a Committee Member over to Rochdale to obtain guidance from their Chairman and then discussed the member's cab fare at Board level. (37)

During the mid-1880's an Investigating Committee was set up to examine 'fees and fares'. It is clear that Mitchell would have preferred to deal with the matter differently, answering written enquiries from Societies as they came in. (38) He was quite capable of exhibiting a Statist 'trust me' mentality, against the associationist forms in which otherwise he was so imbricated. But he did not try to block the investigation. The Committee reported. In November 1884 they listed 12 directors and the amounts they had received in excess of their allowance, and suggested that in future a lump sum of £2,000 be allotted to the directors to be divided up as they saw fit. This idea was rejected. At one General Committee meeting, it got to the point of a motion being passed saying that fees paid to Mitchell on March 3rd 1884 had been correct. (39) A reply to the

Investigating Committee on behalf of the directors was printed and issued to shareholders. (40) Then, an accountant submitted a report showing that Mr. Mitchell had, in fact, been overpaid £1/13/-d on his March 1884 journey to Newtown. It was resolved (with Mitchell staying in the chair) that this amount be refunded by him. The General Committee accepted that they should have appealed to a General Meeting to fix fresh payments to deputations. A special General Meeting was held on 24th January 1885. A leader was published in the *Co-operative News* on January 31st 1885 saying that the directors had indeed failed, in so far as they had not been seen to be fair. New scales were fixed. (41) At the end of the affair, the General Committee resolved that all papers to do with the Investigating Committee be turned over to them. 'Fees and fares' remained as a bite which could always be scratched. Mitchell was still referring to them in 1892. In his Presidential speech to Congress that year, he recalled the Rochdale Pioneers. 'At that time the Committee worked for naught. There was no bother in those days about fees and fares. (Laughter)'. (42) 'This book I hold in my hand is one of the first copies of the rules of the Equitable Pioneers, and the name upon the corner is that of Samuel Ogden, Rochdale, No. 1... But I find at the finish of the rules it says that: "If the auditor does not attend to his duties he is to be fined 2s.6d., and if the delinquent be a salesman or cashier, he is to be fined 1s. A president being late, he was fined 3d., and if he did not come at all, he had to pay 6d. (A voice, "Grand old days")'. (43)

Some of the internal politics of all this can still be picked up, though some of them are bound to be missed by an outsider like me. Mitchell was clearly under attack from particular delegates to the General Committee and to the Quarterly Meetings. These Quarterly Meetings were remarkable occasions. If only we could have a film of one of them, it would be the single most revealing document about Mitchell and the CWS. Up to 600 delegates gathered to discuss, formally to run, this vast working class enterprise. What a way, W.H.

Lever might have remarked, to run a fruit stall, let alone a business empire! They were occasions as remarkable as the cotton and coal 'parliaments' of the same period and the same culture which so impressed the Webbs in *Industrial Democracy* (1897). Working class congress in nineteenth and twentieth century Britain was a major cultural form. At the CWS, grand initiatives jostled with minutiae, principles with personal animosities. Mitchell chaired them all. It was obviously his particular craft.

It is unsurprising that he got criticism as well as accolades. Trouble seemed to come mostly from the Manchester Equitable and the Heckmondwike Societies, via Delegates Pigstone, Redfearn and Crabtree. Fees and fares were only one expression of it. In 1879, the issue of whether the CWS should join the Manchester Chamber of Commerce came up. (44) Crabtree and Pigstone were in favour, Mitchell against. Mitchell's view was that if they had been a mere joint stock company it would have been correct for them to join. But they were not. The Wholesale was not in the business of protecting the interests of private traders, unlike the Chamber, where there were many who had no sympathy for Co-operation. Pigstone (President of Manchester and Salford Equitable Co-operative Society) wanted the CWS to 'take its place in the commercial councils of this great community'. Mitchell wanted it to go on 'acting by itself'. Pigstone heard Mitchell's speech on the subject with 'great pain'. He accused him of making class feeling where none should be. At the Quarterly Meeting Mitchell only just won, losing 112 to 82 votes in Manchester and winning 170 to 112 through the aggregation of votes from Newcastle and London. The CWS had a democratic device whereby they conferred on identical agendas in different centres and then aggregated the votes.

It was James Crabtree (1831-1917) who got under Mitchell's skin more than anyone else, including his opponents the Christian Socialists, Hughes, Greening and Neale. (45) Crabtree had preceded Mitchell as Chairman of the CWS from 1870 to 1874. He had been the main mover in the foundation of the Heckmondwike Society. Crabtree was cautious. He was doubtful about innovations like Co-operative banking, CWS manufacturing, Mitchell's bold ambitions in the merchant shipping world, and extensions such as the opening of a CWS branch in Bristol. He was not the stuff of which entrepreneurs are made, individual or collective. He had resigned from the CWS Board when he became connected with the Heckmondwike Manufacturing Company Ltd., formed in 1873 to take over an old firm of carpet, blanket and rug makers whose business had failed. Perhaps it was this decision, combined with his slowly, slowly temperament, which led him to attack Mitchell so much over the latter's out-of-hours association with the Lancashire and Yorkshire Productive Society. When Mitchell applied to the CWS for a loan in order to cover an overdraft from this undertaking, Crabtree objected. He had a point. The discussion was about whether it was right for Mitchell, in his position, to be applying for loans on behalf of other societies. Mitchell felt his integrity was being questioned. It was at a Quarterly Meeting, he came near to losing his temper:

> 'He had told Mr. Crabtree before he made that statement that there was no personal interest whatever of any kind; then why should Mr. Crabtree continue to make prejudicial statements? (Mr. Crabtree: No). It must be so; it could not have any other effect, and it was impossible for them to have the same regard for their Chairman after these statements as they had before, because they would think he was appropriating

> their money when he was doing nothing of the kind, and he trusted he never should as long as he lived'. (46)

Crabtree defended his conduct in a letter. (47) It was plain that he was not only resentful: there was a real issue at stake. It was a matter, he suggested, of the office not the man. 'We shall not always have Mr. Mitchell in the chair - we may have somebody else in'. Mitchell appealed for trust and confidence. (48) He was having an attack of that characteristic Statist disease of confusing himself with his office - le mouvement c'est moi. A few years before, in the *Co-operative News* in 1875, E.V. Neale had accused the entire CWS enterprise of 'Caesarism'. (49) Crabtree and Mitchell went on niggling, clearly at odds with each other. Following what Crabtree regarded as a 'savage attack' on him, he wrote to the *Co-operative News* saying that Mitchell 'has yet to learn to differ in opinion without differing in feeling, and thus making it a personal matter. It is in this sense I fear his vindictive spirit is calculated to injure innocent persons'. (50) In his memoir of Mitchell in the CWS Annual for 1896, William Maxwell, President of the Scottish CWS, defended his dead friend against feelings which were obviously still alive: 'a pure-minded man... sometimes suspected and doubted by men who were profiting by his unselfish labours'. It is interesting that at the time of his funeral in 1895, rumours about Mitchell being a wealthy man were circulating in Rochdale. Various figures were put about as to the exact sum, from £5,000 to £80,000. 'Now as a matter of fact', commented the *Rochdale Observer*, 'Mr. Mitchell died a poor man'. (51)

Mitchell's relations with the Lancashire and Yorkshire Productive Society were particularly controversial. In 1896 Maxwell provided detailed accounts of them. When Mitchell accepted the job of liquidator the position was hopeless: 'he simply smiled at those who said it was a forlorn hope'. All of the share capital and half the loan capital was gone. Some of the Co-operative Societies holding capital struck it out of their assets, believing it lost. Mitchell began by raising 'special loans' on his own responsibility. These came to £4,000 which, with the overdraft from the CWS Bank, enabled him to keep the Littleborough works going. By August 1894 he was able to pay out the original private and sick burial societies' loans, at 5% compound interest. These amounted to £4,350, leaving a debit balance at that date of £850. Mitchell succeeded in writing up the share capital to its original amount, from £2,640 to £6,600. He never received 'one penny for expenses or remuneration'. When he was voted £20 for expenses in April 1880, he did not take it. It was placed to his credit in the Society's books as loan capital. 'After that time he would not allow the subject of remuneration to be considered at the Society's meetings'. While acting as liquidator, he sold about 16% of the product outside the Co-operative Movement. 'The highest wages were paid to the workers'. (52) After his death the loan standing in his name amounting, with interest, to £41, was paid to his executors. Maxwell's verdict was: 'Comment on such work is useless. It speaks of a hero, a commercial giant - in fact it is unique in the commerce of the land'. (53)

William Maxwell was no slouch. He was a prime mover in the construction of the Shieldhall estate of SCWS productive works. His praise of Mitchell was intimate. But Crabtree's feelings can be understood. They were expressed during years when Mitchell was playing for high stakes, in a competitive casino which Mitchell did not find intimidating. He wanted to win, to be 'thoroughly and completely successful'. Such ambition may explain quite a lot of the attitudes of others towards him, both the working class, Manchester and Heckmondwike colleagues close to him within the Wholesale and the middle class, 'Christian Socialist' idealists at a slightly greater distance, for whom independent plebeian ambition - and the palpable competence which went with it in this case - were problematic.

As Holyoake wrote on page one of his *History of the Rochdale Equitable Pioneers*, defending the working class which was his class too, 'the business habit is not thought to be their forte. The art of creating a large concern, and governing all its complications, is not usually thought to belong to them'. The History was intended as a sustained correction of this view. So too was Mitchell's life.

Mitchell must sometimes have felt that he hardly needed attacks from within the Movement: his agenda in the contest with competition was formidable. For instance, during the years immediately following the case of the Littleborough loan, the question of the CWS owning their own fleet of merchant ships was raised. During the second quarter of 1883, Mitchell needed to explain a loss in the CWS shipping department. (54) This was at a time when he was also keen to expand it, against the caution of a minority of delegates to the Quarterly Meetings. He finally got the go-ahead to buy up to three new boats in March 1884. (55) But not without drawing on his deepest resources of belief and entrepreneurial courage.

The Society was running boats between Hamburg and Goole. They were transporting butter. The CWS had wanted a reduction in transport costs. The private lines had refused, so the CWS started running their own boats. 'Immediately after doing that', Mitchell explained to delegates, 'they came into collision with other shipping interests of long-standing and greater power, *so far as money could give them power* ' (my emphasis). Their opponents reduced their rates from 48/4d. to 30/- a ton, in order to drive the Wholesale off the seas. Instead, the CWS used their size to take the income loss and to let their customers in Co-operative societies have the benefit of lower prices. Whereupon the private traders also reduced their prices on a range of goods, including butter. 'As a gentle hint' said Mitchell, who clearly enjoyed the cut and thrust, 'and to show them that they were quite up to the competition mark, the Wholesale then reduced the (shipping) rates, which affected their competitors. ("Hear, Laughter"). The latter then approached the Society to ask if they could negotiate agreed rates.

Mitchell's buoyancy stemmed from his belief that Co-operators' power of association gave them an edge against private interests. Small and local were not beautiful, so far as he was concerned. His theory was that mobilisation of common hopes and purposes - in huge aggregations - was itself as material as money. Such mobilisation, indeed, constituted labour's capital, enabling members of Co-operative societies to put 'capital', as capitalists called it, in its proper place, which was as a hired servant of labour.

> 'I may tell you this, that there are people on the Eastern side of England who are very large people, and they have said that they will break us down, if it takes them ten years to do it. (A voice, "They can't"). If the co-operators have the pluck of Englishmen, they will say, as the have always said, they may fight for fifty years and they will not break us down. (Cheers) You have overcome as gigantic monopolies as these. It is only a class of monopoly, but it is monopoly of wealth, and you have as large wealth and as large power *within yourselves* (my emphasis) to break down that monopoly as ever you have had before. You are stronger now than you were formerly. You broke down

> hedges, banks, and gates, and though there are iron bars, you will break those down too, I hope. (Cheers)' (56)

This was drawing on an old, eighteenth century tap root of co-operation: countering the monopolists with the people's potentially monopolistic power, enclosing everywhere - the land in general - against petty landlords of corners of the human field. Such tyrants needed cutting down to size. This was a project for which Mitchell needed all the power he could muster, inside himself as well as in the Wholesale. The associational culture in which he had grown up had endowed him and, he thought, all other Co-operators, with a formidable amount of 'power within yourselves'. It was what Max Weber in an earlier context called an 'ethic'.

Before getting closer to this ethic and the political philosophy which went with it, I want to give further voice to some of those who reflected on Mitchell and his project from a greater class distance than the colleagues already quoted. I want to juxtapose some Christian Socialist and Fabian reactions to Mitchell with some more, rather different, contemporary observations of him from within the Movement. This may all seem rather indirect. But it is my contention that the class matrix in which Mitchell's project has been set, before and after his death, has been, in the first place, the main cause of the long concealment of that project. But, at the same time, that matrix has its own importance beyond J.T.W. Mitchell. It needs understanding if the wider history and practice of co-operation is to be advanced.

Selfish, only interested in the dividend; business men not co-operators; materialists not idealists; in need of leading out (educating) into progress; incorrect, in the sense that a child's answer in an exercise book gets marked with a cross rather than a tick: theoretically mistaken; interested in consumption, not production; shopkeepers not community builders; facts and figures, figures and facts, not visions and dreams; incorporated, full of 'middle class values'; at best reformist, at worst capitalist; certainly not revolutionary. To anyone who knows the literature on working class association since 1850 in general or on the Co-operative Movement since 1844 in particular, this will be familiar ground. Its most direct expression in relation to Mitchell has been Backstrom's recent assertion that 'in most ways he reflected the attitudes of the bourgeoisie'. (57)

It is tones of voice which are important. From 1874 to 1902 Ben Jones (1847-1942) was general manager of all departments of the London Branch of the CWS except tea, coffee and cocoa. His father had been a dyer's labourer, his mother a power loom weaver. In 1894, he wrote a huge book, *Co-operative Production*, published by O.U.P. He regarded Mitchell as a father: 'personally, he treated me as if I were a son, and I shall always look back to him with feelings of admiration as a co-operator, and also with feelings of filial affection'. (58) His book is a key source for CWS theory and massive testimony to the fact that there was such a thing. He picked up the tones of voice I am referring to when, for example, he quoted Christian Socialist reaction to the break-up of their producer co-operatives ('workshops') in the mid-1850's:

> 'It has been found very necessary to have some proof that men have foresight and self-denial before they should be encouraged to associate. Working men in general are not fit for association. They come into it with the idea that it is to fill their pockets and lighten their work at once, and that every man is to be his own master' (59)

The second half of the nineteenth century saw a great deal of this. The welcome to co-operation and to working class association more generally during this period was a loud and public one, but it was highly qualified. It was one of those embraces which make breathing difficult. It was, in fact, part of a fight, a fight against particular notions (independent, private, working class notions) and particular potentials inherent in large-scale working class association. The welcome aimed at preventing as much as enabling things to happen.

Thomas Brassey in 1873:

> 'It has seemed to be a belief in co-operative stores, and not altogether avoided in co-operative works, that anyone, without previous knowledge, might be a manager. It would be strange if a man whose life had been spent in manual labour could successfully and instantaneously become a buyer and trade in commodities of which he has hitherto only been a consumer, and much more strange to find one totally unaccustomed to mercantile life who could successfully carry on a large manufacturing concern' (60)

Even at Congress, or especially at Congress until the early 1890's, Bishops, Lords and other would-be patrons were given to utterances of this kind. When I read them I always wish I could see who in the audience was frowning, who nodding.

Lord Reay in 1882:

> 'English co-operators have never boasted that they were going to renovate English society... Co-operation has been the best friend of capital and is, therefore, he strongest ally of the middle class' (61)

By the end of this essay, I hope I will have shown - at least with reference to Mitchell - what partial truth, partial rubbish (but equally important either way) the sheer quantity of this kind of wishful thinking was. (62)

On occasion, the gloves came off. By the early 1890's, the 'idealists' were in retreat within the main organisational centres of the Movement. In January 1892, Judge Hughes, the Christian Socialist, wrote to Holyoake thus:

> 'If I had my way it would have been a much keener attack on that stronghold which the devil has managed to plump down in our midst and which may yet set the good time back for a generation. I had written this time last year to decline the usual gift of the Wholesale Annual,but didn't send it and the book back on Neale's advice. Still I am not sure that the time has not come for taking off the gloves with Mitchell and his tail,who have no faith in co-operation (or anything else) that "goes down deeper than their dinner" ' (63)

No wonder that at the height of arguments with these people, Mitchell felt that the Wholesale was being 'slandered', and that he had to defend it, as at the 1887 and 1891 Congresses, as being as 'high' a form of co-operation as existed 'anywhere on earth'.

Beatrice Webb's gloves were of the choicest kid. On the face of it, she was admiring. Indeed, she regarded the CWS and its Board as 'above corruption'. She admired Mitchell greatly, to the point of 'genius'. She was anxious to praise the CWS in terms familiar to her, namely the political economy of W.S. Jevons. However, as always, her diaries said much more than her theories might allow. During 1889, she was studying the Co-operative Movement. She spent some time in Manchester getting to know the CWS.

> 'Mitchell, Chairman of the CWS, is one of the leading personalities in the Co-operative Movement... a sort of embodiment of the working man customer, intent on getting the whole profit of production, out of the hands of the manufacturer and trader, for the consumer... As the representative of the Wholesale, he is inspired by one idea - the enlargement and increased power of the organisation of which he is the head. He supports himself on the part proceeds of a small woollen business, and draws perhaps 30s. a week from the Wholesale to which he devotes his whole energies. With few

> wants (for he is an old bachelor), he lives in a small lodging, eats copiously of heavy food and drinks freely of tea: no spirits and no tobacco. Corpulent, with a slow bumptious pronunciation of long phrases, melting now and again into a boyish bonhomie... He is a good fellow, and in his inflated way a patriotic citizen... His Board of Directors are entirely subordinate to him: they are corpulent, heavy eaters, but for the most part they are neither more nor less than simple tradesmen... Three or four times I have dined with the Central Board. A higgledy-piggledy dinner; good materials served up coarsely, and shovelled down by the partakers in a way that is not appetising.' (64)

In June 1889, Beatrice attended the Ipswich Co-operative Congress. She was welcomed warmly at the door of the White Horse Inn by Mitchell and others of 'my old friends of the Wholesale'. She experienced the scene inside as 'a happy hunting ground for the social investigator'. Then she moved to the Pickwick Inn and observed how 'at the Co-operative Congress there is an absolute equality: all live together on the freest of terms'. 'It is Sunday evening and we are all assembled in the long coffee room'. Professor Marshall, who had tried to put Beatrice off the idea of writing a book on Co-operation on the grounds that it was not fit work for a woman, had been elected to give the inaugural address that year:

> 'He looks every inch a professor. A small slight man with bushy moustache and long hair, nervous movements, sensitive and unhealthily pallid complexion, and preter-naturally keen and apprehending eyes, the professor has the youthfulness of physical delicacy... Tonight his desire to gain information outweighs his nervous fear of a sleepless night, and he is listening with mingled interest and impatience to the modicum of facts dealt out in the inflated and involved phrases of Mitchell'.

Mitchell, 'raising his sonorous voice and thundering on the table with his fat fist', told Marshall of his beliefs:

> 'having delivered himself of his usual tea party peroration and finding none to dispute his points...(he) relapsed into the enjoyment of highly sugared tea and much-buttered toast; his huge corpulent form, shiny bald head, clean shaven face, exhibiting a full, good-tempered mouth, largely developed jaw and determined chin, so completely affirmed the force of his argument in favour of organised consumption, that it seemed useless to draw from

> him further verbal expressions
> of it.' (65)

So, Mitchell's body was his argument! By such criteria, neo-classical economics must have been thin indeed.

We are dealing here with more than a few private remarks. We are dealing with a kind of acceptance which is, at the same instant, a profound - fastidious, physical and ugly - rejection. We are also dealing with attitudes which have a long history and a wide sociology. We are dealing, in fact, with the discourse within which the history of the Co-operative Movement has been set.

The tones of voice registered here predate the alleged shift from community building to shopkeeping for which the Rochdale phase of Co-operation has been held responsible. From the earliest days of the organised Co-operative Movement in the late 1820's and early 1830's, there was this feeling from some quarters that organised selfishness, with particular reference to stomachs, was destroying the idealism of 'true co-operation'. During this early period, however, the arguments seem to have been about strategy, rather than the class prejudice so evident in Hughes and Webb. (66)

People on a level with Mitchell left images of him very different from the ones we were left with in the Pickwick Inn, Ipswich. They are a pleasure to set down. George Jacob Holyoake (1817-1906) a working class Owenite by origin (like John Watts) was capable of ideological disagreement with Mitchell, but not the kind of physical prejudice quoted above which in ethnic settings would be recognised as racist stereotyping. Holyoake did not like what he saw as the 'grim fanaticism' of temperance advocates. He attacked them at the Co-operative Congress of 1878 in those terms, but hurried to make an exception of Mitchell who 'thinks every advocate is as pleasant as himself' and 'whose face is as radiant as a jubilee'. (67) 'I was in the presence of one of the courtliest, nicest and most-to-be-respected gentleman' (68): 'his kindly and intelligent face at once making him attractive to all who came in contact with him': 'although it cannot be said he was a musician, he was passionately fond of singing...(this) often found expression in his bursting into some of the hymns he knew so well'; 'one of the brightest and happiest men on earth'; 'although his home was almost destitute of domestic comfort... his brightness never forsook him... his racy anecdote, beaming countenance and hearty handshake spoke of contentment and happiness'; 'his general demeanour tolerant in the extreme... never evasive, always courteous and frequently humorous', 'his genial wisdom', 'his presence was hailed with gladness everywhere', 'his beautiful life' (69): 'transparent character', 'the kindling eye, the beaming smile, the rich, cordial tone of his vice', 'a more perfectly transparent and unsuspicious nature could not be found', 'a nameless charm of manner', 'the outshining of a sincere, childlike and generous soul', 'you young people will never forget... the bright look that seemed to light up the School (referring to the Sunday School) (70): 'blameless and Christlike'; 'an indispensable presence', 'perennial smile and amiability of character' (71).

Mitchell's quickness in the old sense of that word, on the platform and as a chairman also struck people close to him. The impression, which comes across from the close quarters of the Movement itself, is not that of the overstuffed receptacle, but rather that of the animated producer, of enthusiasm, what the French would call an animateur. 'Contagious', Maxwell called him.

> 'His energy is unflagging, and the vigour of his mind enables him to accomplish the most arduous tasks... he is a ready speaker, grasps ideas promptly, and has the somewhat rare

> power of expressing his opinions with clearness... His wit loves to play not wound, and he is generous and "religious of his word" '. (72)

One of Robert Halstead's first memories of the Co-operative Movement in the Lancashire town where he came from, was of seeing and hearing Mitchell on the platform, and of his 'vigorous speaking and quick energetic movements... on the platform of our local Co-operative hall. I was too young at that time to realise what he had on his mind to get so excited about'. (73) A correspondent of the *Daily Chronicle* was of the opinion that 'to see Mr. Mitchell at his best you must have been privileged to gain entrance to one of the Quarterly Meetings of the Wholesale in Manchester'. His 'vigour, enthusiasm, shrewdness and wholehearted devotion... were simply elemental in character',

> 'Punctual to the moment, the large, clean-shaven, ruddy-faced man in the chair would strike the gong and call the meeting, usually as large as the House of Commons on a crowded night, to order. There was no opening speech, nothing in the way of palaver. But if the winds arose and the storms came, the Chairman was ready, sometimes with the softest of answers, oftener with a joke or a story that put the hard-headed Northerners into the best of humour, and on occasion with a decisive word which made one wonder what

would happen if the giant really put his foot down. He was the purest embodiment of democracy at the helm conceivable and the co-operators enjoyed and appreciated the way he handled them. The openness and simplicity of it all were transparent. But it was a great exhibition of character, and a most signal instance on the delegates' part of the self-imposed discipline of democracy' (74).

William Maxwell was with Mitchell when he was 'heckled' by the Commissioners of the Royal Commission on Labour, when he appeared as witness for the CWS in 1892. Once again, the imagery is rather different from that used by Beatrice Webb. Maxwell uses language which evokes innocence and enthusiasm rather than bellying 'corpulence':

> 'He surprised some of the gentlemen by the enthusiastic descriptions he gave of the power of co-operation. He gambolled with millions of money in share and loan capital. He jauntily talked of fleets of co-operative steamers. He wrote down buildings and machinery by thousands of pounds annually, till some of his hearers called for proofs of his statements. Balance sheets were handed round immediately'. (75)

All this presence, it was widely agreed, was achieved without self-regard. 'Disinterested ways' (76): 'without a trace of self-seeking' (Hirst Hollowell): 'than whom no more unselfish man ever existed', 'he couldn't be corrupted' (Maxwell): 'I believe if ever there was an unselfish man it was Mr. Mitchell' (77): 'an attitude of simplicity, honest, original and at all times unspoilt by any craving for social distinction or titular decorations': 'I can hear him saying at all times, "I'm only John Mitchell, doing my best for my fellow men", a sort of reincarnation of Abou Ben Adhem' (78). And so on.

Contradictory reactions to Mitchell and his work can never be fashioned into a single truth. Instead, they can be assembled, and then used to tell us what they can about real material conflicts. They lead us into the long conflict, the class struggle, between reformers from above on the one hand and working class associationists on the other. (79) Dominant, inherited views of Mitchell have been the result of the former attempting to diminish the latter. The Webb example is quintessential. There was much more than heavily-buttered toast and well-sugared tea between Beatrice and John Mitchell. The Webb oeuvre on Co-operation - beyond Beatrice's diaries (80) - did a number of things to Mitchell's project: four in fact, and all of them in the interest of their own, rather different concerns. First the Webb work on co-operation suggested that it was admirable but ham-fisted and untheoretical, 'neither more nor less than simple tradesmen', 'good materials served up coarsely'. Secondly, the Webb work suggested that Mitchell and the CWS were unconsciously, as it were spontaneously, Jevonian: that is to say that they unwittingly subscribed to a *political economy*. This is wrong already: Mitchell and the CWS worked more within a moral economy, tending towards a social economy tradition. The political economy which the Mitchell/CWS practice underwrote, the Webbs thought, showed how 'it was in recognised "utility", or specific demand, that lay the dominating and determining factor of exchange value'. 'The Co-operative Movement of Great Britain... perhaps because it was genuinely of working class origin, achieved without intending' (81). Thirdly the Webb view suggested that the CWS had shown that productive co-operation was an unscientific Shangri-La, and that "Consumers' Co-operation" was the only way forward. There was, in their view, to be a division of labour between people as citizens, people as producers and people as consumers. The Co-operative Movement was to be corralled into the consumer section. As I hope to show, Mitchell's ambition was, on the contrary, to shepherd all these functions into one Co-operative Movement in order to bring consumers and producers, governors and governed, face to face in a single association. Fourthly, and perhaps most important of all, Beatrice offered herself - and to a degree was accepted by inside CWS interpreters such as Percy Redfern - as the theorist articulating the CWS/Mitchell side of the late nineteenth century struggle over co-operation. In doing so, she tried to dump the State on top of it. In her book on *The Co-operative Movement* (lst edition 1891, going into 4 editions before 1899 and 3 reprints before 1910) Beatrice argued that the trade union and co-operative movements, though bringing valuable 'moral reform', needed to be supplemented by socialist legislation.

This was fine, provided it is recognised as more Beatrice's project than Mitchell's. The State was to be staffed by collectivist experts, trained through institutions like the L.S.E. Its construction was to constitute a break, a new civilisation. Working class associations were fine, heroic. No one has chronicled them in more loving detail than the Webbs. But there was to be a next stage beyond them, in which the initiative would shift to 'social scientists'. These were not the Owenite and working class critics of political economy who coined the phrase 'social science' earlier in the nineteenth century. They were to be a new cadre of professionals with, no doubt, similar reactions to places like the Pickwick Inn and with gatherings characteristically rather different form the 'absolute equality, all live together on the freest of terms' which Beatrice observed at Co-operative Congress. Working class associations would have their place, but many of their inventions and much of their culture - for that is what it was - would come to look 'primitive' from a professional point of view, just like the Quarterly Meetings of the CWS from 1874 to 1895. To the extent that it contributed to the aborting of an emergent critique of the State from Labour's point of view, this may have been the Webbs' most crippling legacy to the autonomy and potential originality of the Co-operative Movement's contribution to working class socialism in our time. For Mitchell and his ilk, working people doing it for themselves - the old 'who does what?' question of craft unionism - were all important. To change who did what: that was the project. As I hope to show by getting back behind the Webbs, Mitchell was an egalitarian with gigantic ambition. But the ambition was for his own association, its ethic and all its federated forms, not for any actually existing State.

I will complete this section with two episodes to bear in mind while reading the rest of this essay. The first is Robert Owen writing in the *New Moral World* in 1837. 'The working classes never did direct any permanently successful operations... Whenever the working classes have attempted any complicated, important measure that required unity, patience, and perseverance to bring it to a successful issue they have failed in every instance as soon as they have taken the direction of it'. (82)

The second is a Rochdale Pioneer making a presentation to Edward Vansittart Neale in May 1891. At this event, Abraham Greenwood cast his mind back forty years, to a day in 1851 when Christian Socialists were visiting the Rochdale Flour Mill. The image which stuck in his mind and which he recalled, to laughter, was that of the gentlemen taking their coats off and turning them inside out, lest they got dirty. (83)

And two final encores. Judge Hughes: 'No faith in co-operation or anything else that goes down deeper than their dinner'. Lord Reay: 'English co-operators never boasted that they were going to renovate English society'. We shall see.

IV

Not long before he died, Mitchell addressed a meeting at an exhibition of Co-operative products in Manchester.

He said:

> 'Our Movement was no longer a theory, it was a great fact, the best outcome of civilisation, and an embodiment of Christianity in trade. The political economists of the last century made selfish individualism the basis of commerce and taught that men should compete with one another for their own good. Co-operation taught that men should work together for the good of the whole community, that wealth should not be confined to a few, but distributed for the benefit of the entire population. The present condition of things in the social and industrial world was a scandal to so-called civilisation. A few were living in palaces, clothed in silk and velvet, and thousands of men, women and children were half starved and in rags. Co-operation would bring to the masses of the people the comforts which heaven designed them to enjoy in this world'. (84)

In 1879, he told a public meeting at Congress that his ambition was no less than 'to create a new order of things', 'to change the world'. (85) This was his language in front of the Royal Commission on Labour during the early 1890's too. He wanted 'a new state of things'. In 1874, the year that his work became Manchester/CWS centred rather than Rochdale centred, he went to the annual gathering of the Accrington and Church Industrial Co-operative Society. He used the occasion to look closely at their yearly statement and to get excited about the communal prospect it opened up for the whole of Accrington. Over the preceding fifteen years, he observed, they had created a profit exceeding £100,000. Properly invested within the Society, he thought, that might have employed 500 of their members, 'receiving amongst themselves the profits of their own industry',

> 'He was anxious that the lever which the working classes now had in their hands should be employed not to make other men rich, whilst they (the workers) labour and toil and sweat for a bare existence, but to secure for them a perpetual redemption from all acts of slavery and tyranny... Capital was not the enemy of the working man: it was his friend. He wished them to use it for their own elevation and the good of their children. He asked why should not they conduct productive societies as well as distributive and thus secure to themselves the profits made in those manufacturing

> concerns. There was no reason why twenty years hence, Accrington should not be one gigantic productive concern, and that the profits should be divided amongst the whole inhabitants of the town'. (86)

'Perpetual redemption from all acts of slavery and tyranny'; a city as a gigantic productive concern with profits equally divided among everyone; the scandal of misery in a world where the comforts which heaven 'designed them to enjoy' were materially available to all, given proper social arrangements... this was a Radical/Owenite stance. And in Mitchell's case, as in that of Dr. John Watts, the same set of feelings was evident which I would call their 'if only...' mentality. There was no reason why not, and in twenty years time too, if only... if only they retained the surplus of their labour for themselves. 'And if everybody will carry out our principle, I believe most emphatically that we shall reconcile the interests of capital, labour and consumption in a manner the world has never seen before'. (87) 'If the trade of this country could be carried on solely by co-operation, in fifty years time the Society could buy up the whole of the land in England'. 'That was no exaggerated theory, but practical fact'. (88) 'Let them look forward to that time. He did not believe it to be a Utopian idea. He believed it to be a practical idea of trade that they should secure to themselves the great benefits both of import, manufacturing, merchanting and banking'. (89)

V

Mitchell's vision may, for convenience, be divided into four parts. The first will centre on movement, the second on class, the third on system, and the final one on politics.

i. *The movement and the ethic of association.*

'Our movement was no longer a theory. It was a great fact.'

Before looking at Mitchell through other people's eyes, we left him in Rochdale. He had joined the Sunday School, the Congregational, the Temperance and the Equitable Pioneers movements.

He joined the Rochdale Equitable Pioneers in 1853. His grandfather had been a member of the 'Co-operative shop' at no. 15 Toad Lane which failed 'on account of its giving credit to members', and had lost money in that failure. (90) At Mitchell's funeral, a wreath arrived from Mr. George Healy J.P. of Windermere, the only survivor of the original 28. By 1855, Mitchell was a Committee Member. He was elected Secretary in 1857. (91) By October 1868, he was Treasurer of the R.E.P.S. Education Department of which the Minute Book for 1867-8 records him attending 117 out of a possible 155 meetings and being late on 4 occasions.

Mitchell became an early member of the Co-operative Manufacturing Society at Mitchell Hey, from the mid-1850's through to the 1860's, and Chairman of the Directors there for a number of years. Initially, the 1400 shareholders from the Rochdale Society tried profit sharing with the 300 workers in this cotton mill. But jealousy and friction entered in. (92) After a long and bitter controversy, and by a majority of 3 to 1, the bonus was abolished in 1862. 'There is reason to believe', wrote 'Prospero' during the 1920's, that Mitchell himself proposed the majority motion at that time, 'on practical grounds... he had not formulated any theory'. There is evidence of religious or at least denominational dimensions to the controversy, with Secularists, Unitarians and Churchmen supporting the bonus and Methodists and Congregationalists forming a 'united party' against it. (93)

Mitchell's 'positions' on key issues in the Movement were not positions in the sense that political people use the word: they were experiences in context, coming out of his life as well as his head. When discussing bonus to labour, he would recall his experience as a child factory worker, and wonder what difference it would have made. Finding formulae which enabled Societies to achieve continuity - the reiterated contrast made by Mitchell between the first half of the nineteenth century and the second - made the difference for him, in lived family experience, between poverty and comfort. During the middle years of the century, he was also closely associated with the Rochdale Corn Mill Society; acted as the representative of the Pioneers at meetings of the Lancashire and Yorkshire Railway Company; and was particularly involved with the Education Committee of the Pioneers' Society. This was the only aspect of the R.E.P.S.'s work with which he remained 'intimately connected' long after concentrating his energies on the CWS. (94)

For 21 years Mitchell was also Honorary Secretary to the Science and Art Classes in Rochdale, a national (South Kensington Department) source of funds to which the Co-op in Rochdale affiliated. So he knew the Co-operative Movement, just like he knew the Sunday School movement for which he would leave Congress early when it was in distant places (as in Plymouth in 1886), in order to be in his place in Milton Chapel punctually on Sunday morning. The movement was not an adjunct to him, 'my club' in a different class discourse, or a sector of his life as in 'the voluntary sector'. It was his culture, the medium in which he grew. Using the *Co-operative News* to discover his whereabouts, his months of January to mid-February 1886 looked like this: Jan 16, Central Board Meeting, N-W Section, Manchester; Jan 20, Festival, Doncaster; Jan 23, Soiree, Eccles ; Jan 27, Annual Festival, Lincoln; Feb 1, meeting of Manchester Ship Canal Co., Manchester; Feb 6, General Board Meeting of Co-operative Newspaper Society, Manchester and Annual Tea Party, Staithwaite; Feb 9, Coming-of-Age celebrations, Aspatria; Feb 13, Soiree, Rawtenstall. Looking at the CWS Minute Books for 1883-4, there were sub-Committees responsible to the General Committee on Finance, Grocery, Drapery, Shipping and Production. On each of these the G.C. had 5 members, and Mitchell was ex-officio, as the Chairman, on each of them. So that in January 1884 his meetings were as follows: Grocery Jan 8th-10th, Drapery Jan 9th, Shipping same day, Productive Jan 10th, Property Jan 7th, Finance Jan 8th. He also attended the Newcastle Committee on Jan 3rd and the London one on Jan 5th. This was a way of life, not leisure, not work, but a culture. Through such means, Mitchell - in a key phrase of Maxwell's - 'governed himself'. He knew that these associational forms - means of production of labour's own labour power, if labour was ever to own its power - would have to be his class's specific resource if ever they were to be able to achieve their project as interpreted by Mitchell, against all comers.

He stood for 'rationality' in the Weberian sense, but for a specifically working class (but universal not subaltern) rationality. Regularity, clearly articulated ends, deliberately chosen means, ruthless exclusion of tempting sideshows (e.g. independent producer co-operatives), redemption through federation not vertical integration (as a good Congregationalist) in one big association... all these describe Mitchell's project. He was, of course, Protestant, not to say Puritan. He shared the old preference for kinds of romance other than fiction, in his case facts and figures. "Talk of figures being 'dry'! - why they were more interesting and wonderful than any novel." (95) He was disinterested in personal accumulation and, therefore, like Weber's capitalists, good at social accumulation.

He cut out domesticity and drink. At one point he referred to Co-operators as 'peculiar people'. (96) It is tempting to see his project - Deacon of Milton Chapel - as another representation for labour, of that fecund upside-down side of the seventeenth century bourgeois revolution which Christopher Hill has recently made part of our history. Mitchell thought he was dealing not with his own dinner, but with 'the most Christian principle in the world. It was a divine principle' (97).

The confidence of this conviction might explain why middle class improvers were compelled either to miss altogether, or to despise and attack, Mitchell's project. They could not afford by then, as it were, to do anything else. It was not just a matter of Mitchell, but also of the historical context. In the developed conditions of labour associating within, but also reaching out beyond, late nineteenth and early twentieth century capitalism in Britain, Mitchell's could be an *inclusive* rationality, going for the universal. No wonder there had to be a Royal Commission *on Labour* during the early 1890's, and no wonder it was the setting in which Mitchell was goaded into stating his views at their best. He was much nicer to the Christian Socialists than they were to him. He was an eirenic character, with the confidence and in the class context *which could afford to include*. People noticed how he met sectarianism with a smile. (98) By the end of the nineteenth century, rationality and improvement from above could not afford even to appear to be inclusive. By then, there had to be limits to mutuality. Setting such limits was what private competition and public legislation was largely about during this period. There was a great deal of interest at this time, and ever since, vested in the *enclosure* of what threatened to become public, namely large numbers of working people associating democratically in order to change the world. Exclusivity was essential. Otherwise Samuel Smiles's dictum in *Self Help* (1859) that 'what some men are, all might without difficulty become' (99) might be taken too seriously. Serious liberalism, which Holyoake called 'deliberate liberalism', had to be rolled back.

This is what the discourse in and against the Co-operative Movement by its patrons in Mitchell's day was about. A space had to be kept for masters, for Authority, against a Movement which, for all its faults and failings, was experimenting with new spaces, new ways of governing large-scale attempts 'to arrange the powers of production, distribution, education, and government'. (100) Hence the terms upon which, for instance, General Booth could advocate co-operation as central to the solution of the social problem in *In Darkest England and the Way Out* (1890). One of his most important experiments was to be a Co-operative Farm. 'I should propose to renew the experiment of Mr. E.T. Craig, which he found worked so successfully at Ralahine'. (101) At the same time, Booth had definite views on democracy within production:

> 'Management signifies government, and government implies authority, and authority is the last thing which co-operators of the Utopian order are willing to recognise as an essential element to the success of their schemes The Co-operative Institution which is governed on parliamentary principles, with unlimited right of debate and right of obstruction, will never be able to compete successfully with institutions which are directed by a single brain wielding the united resources of a disciplined and obedient army of workers. Hence, to make co-operation a success, you must super-add to the principle of consent the principle of authority'. (102)

'Institutions... directed by a single brain wielding the united resources of a disciplined and obedient army of workers' - this is more redolent of the power-crazed enemies of Dr. Who and other space avengers than of associational culture during the second half of the nineteenth century. Nor did Mitchell have a claque of Time Lords to back him up at CWS Quarterlies. Self-reliance was not about hierarchies of dependence: Congregationalists hired and fired their own priests. Leaders within this associational culture often pondered these matters. When naming one of the engines 'Equality' - the other one was called 'Fraternity' - in the new CWS Flour Mills at Dunston-on-Tyne in 1891 (103), Thomas Burt MP told how Ruskin had thought that the French revolutionaries had made one big mistake. They had left 'Paternity' out of their triad of principles, 'as the representative of authority'. Burt was not sure about this, but he did think that 'forward movement' needed authority, to be orderly as well as progressive, and that Maxwell and Mitchell and the Wholesale Movement had it.

> 'I do not mean that we are to be governed by despotism, but until the time comes when every man can govern himself - and we know that time will come bye and bye - it is necessary that there should be authority somewhere... My friends, the presidents of the Co-operative Wholesale Societies, Mr. Mitchell, Mr. Maxwell, and others, can report real progress'.

The system which produced Mitchell and which he was trying to multiply was more egalitarian than Ruskin's. Admittedly, it would be hard to be less so. It was concerned with 'arranging powers' towards the time when every person could, in and through association, govern himself. One huge caveat must be entered here, though it will have become apparent to today's readers already: the language, though not the entire project as we shall see, was in male terms.

In Mitchell's time, the thrust towards universality was strong: the working class was to become its own employer. The Movement would move through education, biscuits, newspapers, merchant ships, etc. into the National Debt, the railways and everything else. It constituted a Society or set of Societies which were capable of becoming society itself. Such Societies constituted a world, a way of life and, through Co-operative insurance and the funeral service, a way of death too. There was much to gain from it for many thousands of working people who lived and died differently because it was there. When he was giving his testimony to the Royal Commission on Labour, Mitchell listed some of the advantages as steadier work, steadier wages, greater continuity of work, full and friendly dealing with trade unions, a minimum of disputes. (104) Beyond that, bespoke production for use, for an organised, articulate market (the local Societies) was an implicit, but actual, critique of the commodity form itself. Beyond that, a *Daily Chronicle* correspondent suggested on Mitchell's death that,

> 'To him, the Wholesale Society and the Co-operative Movement was not merely "a state within a state", but the very kernel of the state itself. For did it not embody the active habitual working of the principle by which states live and grow? Public service, and the welfare of "the body politic" - a favourite phrase of his - as the condition of individual

> progress, this was Mr. Mitchell's civic gospel and co-operative faith'. (105)

'The active habitual working of the principle by which states live and grow', a 'civic gospel and co-operative faith': the correspondent may have been nearer the mark than Judge Hughes' 'no faith in co-operation (or anything else) that "goes down deeper than their dinner" .

ii. *The class, and equality among human beings.*

Mitchell was very class conscious. He was in no doubt that 'as long as there were two classes in the community - capitalists and labourers - trade unions would be necessary'. (106) He wanted the Unions to bank with the Wholesale, so that they 'might make a beginning in co-operative industry'. He was proud of his class, insistent on class and the dignity of labour - 'in co-operation', he told Congress at Newcastle in 1880, 'they dignified labour'. It is not hard to imagine the delegate from Rochdale's feelings when he went to the first of the new series of Co-operative Congresses in the West End of London in 1869, at the Society of Arts. It was a 'society function': all those gentlemen's coats the right way out, no flour please: and Ladies too, no beerhouse keepers. At this time the CWS, such as it was, held meetings in its back street warehouse, 'the delegates finding rough seats on boards laid across barrels'. (107) Twenty years later, when Mitchell and three other Rochdale Pioneers assumed the Presidency of Congress, for the first time dispensing with outsiders, (the custom was to have a different President on each day), the feeling of proud takeover was palpable: as the *Rochdale Observer* recorded it: 'Co-operation has got beyond the need of patronage'. (108)

Mitchell's performance in front of the Royal Commission on Labour, also in 1892, was poised and rooted. He took the Commissioners right through the nineteenth century history of the Co-operative Movement, supplying appendices listing the 260 societies already there in 1830. 'The ideas of the earlier co-operators', he suggested, 'were rather on the lines of a commune in which there should be no individual profit, but that all members of the community should work in the interests of all'. The CWS's present 'complete system' was only a materialisation of such ideas. Mitchell was in no mood to give the credit for these historic initiatives in 'associated effort' to anyone - including Robert Owen - to anyone but working class people. The CWS was, he said, 'primarily working class'. He then produced a table of the 1,459 Co-operative Societies which were in this association of 'federal production'. These

> 'are entirely working class societies. According to a Return obtained by the Co-operative Union a few years ago, there were only about 2% of members in receipt of £150 a year. Though, in some town Societies, there might perhaps be 5%, the lack of any such members in the country Societies leaves the average as before stated' (109)

Mitchell wanted to 'prevent the accumulation of wealth in any particular channel'. There was to be 'a universal distribution of wealth'. 'What we wanted to accomplish by co-operation was absolute equality in the distribution of wealth, though that hardly seemed possible' (110). Because it did not, in Mitchell's view, constitute a particular, privileged channel, but rather 'the people' (only once have I found him calling them 'the masses', and then it was 'the masses of the people'), the CWS system was to be one of free flow. Its social position was such that 'all the advantages shall flow in the direction of the body politic ', rather than in the direction of a privileged group.

Thus, redistribution of wealth would happen but not by law. Active agency by the state-as-subject would turn the people into objects rather than the subjects of the social sentence they should properly be. The project was, in good part, *about agency*. How changes happened from working people's point of view was a big part of what changes were. The federal aggregate of Wholesale and local Societies was to be the agent, through all the 'qualities that constitute a good man', self-government through thrift, industry and sobriety.

The project was gigantic. Sharing a platform with Tom Mann in Bristol in 1893, Mitchell expressed it thus:

> 'We want to put the profits of trade into the pockets of the people, not a section of them but the entire community. Until the people get hold of trade profits they will never be able to undertake the productive business of the world. Mr. Carnegie of America said that a thousand pounds in the hands of one person would do more good to the community than a thousand persons owning a pound apiece. That was absolutely untrue. It would be better still if the £700,000,000 of the British Debt were owned by the 40,000,000 of British people, than to belong to a small section of the community. Co-operators want to use the best means to get the entire wealth of this country, land and

> everything else, into the possession of the entire body politic'. (111)

Cultural equality, through education, co-operative occasion and so on, was important to Mitchell. A high proportion of his speeches reported in the *Co-operative News* can be read as protestant addresses to working people to feel equal in situations of great hierarchy, a bit like Adam Michnik's exhortations to Solidarity members in Poland to feel free even though they knew their wider situation was one of great repression. The Co-operative Movement in the second half of the nineteenth century in Britain may be seen as a sustained critique of internalised subalternity among working people: credit, for instance, was a power relation to be avoided where possible. 'Why', asked Mitchell at the annual meeting of the Oldham Equitable Co-operative Society on January 15th 1876, 'why should the children of any of those whom he saw before him have an inferior education to the Queen upon the throne? (Hear, hear)'.

> 'Let them have confidence in themselves and in each other; let them promote the diffusion of that knowledge and the boon of that education which would drive away superstition and extinguish suspicion and jealousy, and they would have that bond of united interest which no power on earth could break asunder - they could free themselves from the toil and misery which oppressed them; they could make for themselves a heaven upon earth' (112).

Yet Mitchell was not a romantic: for him, self-realisation lay in being a servant to the cause of 'heaven upon earth' which, in his own eyes, he remained all his life. There was nothing demeaning in that. An insistence on fundamental sameness among humans was very important to Mitchell's thought. To understand this, we need to know much more about the Congregationalism which was so important to him, and important in the formation of many male working class associationists, for instance in the Brotherhood and Pleasant Sunday Afternoon movements, during the late nineteenth and early twentieth centuries. His thought was probably at least as much a theology as was that of the post-Frederick Denison Maurice Christian Socialists. 'God made all men alike', he said in a speech which was really a sermon on the first day of the Carlisle Congress of 1887. He would insist upon a commonality which was so strong that it would contain rather than be contained by divisions of labour. The notion of a 'common bond' was repeated. 'They wanted all co-operators to be bound in one common bond, to live, to work together, having one common interest, because it was only that common interest which would secure that kind of union which would be effective in binding the body politic for the purpose of promoting a great and glorious cause'. (113)

iii. *System, complete co-operation, and no new capitalists.*

For Mitchell, humanity was realised in association as much as in production narrowly understood. His idea of human fulfilment was not individual, and not tied to creativity at the points of material production, and less intrinsically gendered than some socialisms - in the conditions of his day - in so far as *membership* rather than *going-to-work* was to be the channel through which the value of labour was to be (universally) shared. The hero, as it were, was not the male factory worker or, for that matter, the creative artist. Membership was unlimited. In his project, there was a notion of what we might call socialisation-for-labour which could, he hoped, include differentiation at work. Service to a system - a system of 'complete co-operation' - within which, because it was complete, there would be no class interests, was to include and override divisions of labour at work. This system, he thought, was already in place: all it had to do was to grow. Complete loyalty could thus be called for. There are echoes here of both Owenite and Soviet Communist mentalities: it is at this point that the line between theoretical commitment to the communitarian idea in Mitchell's head and organisational (CWS) self-interest (Co-operation in One Country), not to say pigheadedness, is at its thinnest.

When asked in front of the Royal Commission on Labour why the CWS did not follow 'the generally recognised principle of co-operators, that the societies shall divide the fund known as profit equitably between the capitalist, the worker and the purchaser', Mitchell replied that they did but in a different way, through members' purchase of goods. 'And thus, if you get the combination of shoemaker, joiner, and every other artisan class combined in a common bond, everybody gets a share of his own and other persons' productions, because they strengthen the business by the trade which they give to it'.

Divisions of labour within the work place (and payment of wages) characteristic of large-scale industry were tolerated within the CWS system in ways which subsequent socialists have found scandalous. This has been one of the sources of the lingering smell attaching to Mitchell's memory. Indeed modern divisions of labour were championed within the CWS in ways which made men like Ben Jones close cousins of the Fabian collectivists who admired them so. There was an unsentimental determination not to be driven to the wall by private competitors through refusal to use the production methods characteristic of large-scale industry. Ben Jones was quite explicit about this in *Co-operative Production* (1894), as was Mitchell's successor at the Wholesale, Thomas Tweddell from Newcastle.

'The era in which it was possible for a few men to profitably engage in manufacturing operations is fast becoming traditional. In all the principal trades, and in many of the smaller ones, the drift is irresistible in the direction of concentration. For good or ill, we have entered an era of big capitals, operating through gigantic factories, these again equipped with perfect tools, manned by well-drilled armies of men, and forming part only of perfect and far-reaching organisations. If that has been the tendency in the past, it will more than ever by the tendency in the future, for Nature is democratic in her methods, and refuses to work cheaply for the few. Co-operators must learn from these facts that if they are to win permanent success in manufacturing industry, they will have to enlist the aid of large capital and the most perfect organisation. And these auxiliaries hitherto have ranged themselves rather on the side of powerful federations of consumers than on the side of the self-governing, profit-sharing workshop. Indeed that institution has seldom been

> able to command either the capital, the power of cohesion, the faculty of organisation, or one of the essentials of permanence or success, and to seek to supplant the modern capitalist by its means is, to my mind, like opposing a pop gun to the rifled ordnance of the Elswick works' (114).

Supplanting the modern capitalist, in these kinds of working class accents, might well send a shiver down the spine of the most liberal minded, middle class co-operative patrons. 'The rifled ordnance of the Elswick works' indeed! There was, of course, serious argument about co-operative production taking place at this time, to which I have already alluded. It was between the 'Christian Socialist' advocacy of self-governing workshops (with bonus-to-labour, profit sharing etc.) and the CWS notion of *all* production being carried on in large-scale factories governed by the CWS General Committee, the CWS itself being owned and controlled as a federation of local Co-operative Societies. In the CWS system, the benefits of co-operation were to be realised by the worker-as-member (along with all other members) rather than by the worker as producer in his own, self-governing workshop. This was a serious debate, both sides of which are still relevant to anyone interested in the connections which complex co-operation in an era of large-scale industry will require. In this essay, I want to insist on two things: first that the Mitchell/CWS - sometimes known as 'federalist' - side was a serious argument, an ideal, even a theory. History has not, so far, allowed it to be. Secondly, to return to an earlier theme, that in Mitchell's day the conflict was a North-South one; more seriously, it was one between different class attitudes and allegiances.

Edward Owen Greening was a leader of the Southern, Christian Socialist, anti-CWS camp. In 1889, he gave a lecture on his version of 'Complete Co-operation'. At this time, Greening was pleased with himself and with his Labour Association's advocacy of 'the essential principle of co-partnership' against the CWS. He told how he was visiting Leicester some time after an infamous strike by CWS workers against their own Society. In 1887, 60 or 70 workers from the CWS shoe works had applied to the Labour Association for advice on starting a schismatic Society of their own. Greening and friends 'took the trouble' to procure the rules of M. Godin's "Familstere" and to translate them into English 'omitting those parts which an Englishman would not understand or appreciate'. The New Leicester Co-operative Boot Factory had done well, thought Greening, out-pacing the CWS works. This is how he told it:

> 'When I went into that workshop... I saw the men at work, and I saw everywhere the evidence of the wonderful results of the reconciliation of capital and labour. For instance, there was one man stamping out those ornamental fringes they put round the top of ladies' boots, "gimping", I think they call it, by swinging round an immense lever; and he was swinging it round at a tremendous rate. He never stopped all the time I was talking to him. I said, "You are working very hard; don't you stop that all day?". He said, "No; in the Wholesale Society they have got a steam engine

> to do this work, and I have got to get as many dozen a day done by this machine as their steam engine turns out, so I can't stop till I've got my number". You could see the reason for it. His heart was in his work'. (115)

I cannot help imagining Thomas Tweddell or Mitchell asking where else this worker's heart might be in a couple of years' time, if the independent Society failed to put in modern machinery. Nor would Mitchell have read Greening's boast about return on capital in the same light. Whereas the CWS was receiving 3 to 3.5% interest on capital in their works, the new Leicester Factory was, apparently, paying 20% on capital. 'So the capitalists don't suffer', said Greening in his lecture. But that was not what Mitchell and Tweddell meant by reconciliation of the interests of labour and capital.

Mitchell told the Royal Commission on Labour that 'we endeavour to conduct our productive establishments with the highest regard to efficiency of workmanship, combined with sufficient remuneration and comfort of the worker... the best goods, made under the best conditions'. But I have not found him talking so hardheartedly about the division of labour as Thomas Tweddell or Ben Jones. A research project is needed on the conduct of the CWS Productive works in Mitchell's time and after, starting with the biscuit factory at Crumpsall (1873-1986). I have been through the relevant CWS Minutes, and made a sad visit to Crumpsall in search of records during the summer before it closed. Details, I suspect, will have to come from local newspapers. It is perhaps interesting that, on his death, the Chartist, Secularist Thomas Hayes from Failsworth - appointed first Manager at Crumpsall in 1873 - was celebrated as that 'rare type of democrat who combined great activity for the co-operative movement with the daily practice of its central principle in his everyday life'. It may be indicative of a slightly softer attitude in Mitchell than in Tweddell that, on Hayes's death in 1912, it was alleged that Mitchell had said that he was appointed 'not because of his knowledge of the bakery business but because of his sincerity, industriousness and reliability. (116) And there are signs in subsequent Productive Committee Minutes of conflicts at Crumpsall between the imperatives of productivity and softer, co-operative ways. (117)

There was trouble at the Leicester Shoe Works in 1886-7. This led to the fiercest period of dispute between the Christian Socialists and the Mitchell/CWS system. Employees at the CWS factory in Leicester had complained of low wages, in letters to the *Co-operative News*. They also complained that work of an inferior type was being put out to Enderby, in a form of sub-contracting (sweating). Mitchell stuck to the constitutional forms of CWS government, demanding loyalty in a strike which was obviously embarrassing to one for whom (as later in the Soviet Union) strikes were seen as literally incredible. How can a worker strike against himself? He wanted 'authorised statements' not letters of complaint. He tried, too hard, to keep the strike out of Committee reports and, therefore, not discussed at Quarterly Meetings. He set up a sub-group of the CWS Committee to hear complaints. This was unacceptable to protagonists of the strikers such as Edward Owen Greening who wanted a committee of investigation independent of the CWS. Such independence, in anything, went against Mitchell's ideas. It would be to go outside the system. How was it possible to be independent of a body of which one was a member? Thus, while he welcomed trade unions, he refused to concede to workers on CWS ships the right to control recruitment of crews and disciplinary procedures. He wanted to pay Union rates. But he also wanted the CWS committee, as servants in a common bond, to control their own servants in the Productive Works without any loss of autonomy to a body outside the system, whether trade union or otherwise. (118)

Mitchell was angry when the clickers and riveters in Leicester declined to state their case to the CWS Committee: 'was that a respectful way in which to treat the Committee who were their masters having engaged them in the name of the delegates?' (119) Acting in the name of the delegates obviously meant being entitled to ask for complete loyalty to the Committee, within a closed system (a community) of which all were - or at least could be - members. 'The Committee desired and endeavoured to treat all their servants with the greatest respect and consideration possible, but if the delegates came to the Quarterly Meetings and set the authority of the Committee on one side, then the Committee could have no control over their servants'. All within the CWS system were to be masters of each in order to be servants of all, servants of all in order to be masters of each. This could not be expressed in a system of workers' control. (120)

Unity and loyalty were paramount Mitchell values, stronger even than their subsequent expression among working class people in twentieth century Labour Party politics. Concentration of trade in a single channel was his dream:

> 'My desire is that the profits of all trade, all industry, all distribution, all commerce, all importation, all banking and money dealing, should fall back again into the hands of the whole people. If co-operators will manage their enterprises in such a way as to concentrate all their trade in one channel, I am certain that this can be accomplished'. (121)

Anything less than this would be to 'squander' possibility. It was important that no money should leak from the system, 'all co-operative money would be gathered up to be used purely for co-operative purposes'. That was the point of the bank. (122) It was important too that there should be 'an absolute faithfulness' by Societies to their own productive works. This was a continuation of the old tactic of exclusive dealing. (123) Loyalty was demanded from Societies to the Wholesale and from members to Societies: it has lingered in Co-op advertisements ever since. Thomas Woolfenden clearly did not like it when he got a letter from the Committee of the Rochdale Equitable Pioneers Society on April 16th 1881 telling him, that over the previous four quarters, his purchases from the Society had been less than the minimum fixed in the Rules. His case, he was told, was an 'aggravated one' because he was a member of the Educational Committee and a CWS representative. He was asked for an explanation. On April 20th, he gave it. (124) 'From a variety of causes I have not done so much as usual but I need not enter into that here except to say that, if you kept a better butter, I should do more in that alone than would meet the requirements of the rule. Mrs. Woolfenden prefers the best Kiel Butter which we get at the bottom of the Walk which is better than yours at the same price. I could put up with yours, but she cannot'.

But Thomas Woolfenden had has pride. He wasn't going to grovel in order to keep his offices in the Society,

> 'which I have not sought and which I am ready to give up at any time the members may think fit: if this is not satisfactory and if you wish to take advantage of this my first breach of the rule I do not grudge the pleasure. My only regret will be in parting company with an institution which with all its faults I regard

> as the most potent influence in raising the social condition of the class to which I belong more particularly to its educational appliances'.

For Mitchell, means were united with ends *through the movement,* with all its constitutional inventions and disciplines. If you did not take the movement seriously (despising the store) as a way of life rather than as an idea, and as a real life association of large numbers of disagreeing, and sometimes disagreeable, working people, then you did not take Mitchell seriously. It was through active membership of a common movement, based upon thousands of horizontal links of federation, that the person, the member, was to achieve an equitable share of (dividend in, plus democratic control over) the rationalities of co-operative production, distribution and exchange. As a servant, the member might have to obey, say, the Productive Committee of the CWS, but as fellow servants in a common system, the members of such a Committee had a different call on the loyalty of the member than a private, capitalist, irresponsible, unelected tyrant. 'We are, of course, subject to strikes and trade disputes, but liability to these is reduced to a minimum because the Committee are not at all times accessible to the work people in case they have any representations to make and to discuss matters with them', said Mitchell to the Royal Commission in 1892. It was through active membership of a movement that the producer and the consumer came face to face, as the same person. In a complex society, direct relations required complex forms: membership of one or another could not but be messy. It was held to be advisable that, while employees as Co-operators should control the Movement, they should not, as workers, control the works, or even (as employees) the shop. If they did, vested interests would grow up. To the extent that the works or the shop prospered, those exclusively controlling and profiting from them would become capitalists or 'gentlemen who would get rich out of co-operators and then we should have to begin the work of co-operation again' (125). None of this is to suggest that because this was the vision, all of it would be delivered. Not being an island entire to itself, the CWS was vulnerable to all the deformations indicated in the laws of (bourgeois) sociology. 'We encourage all our work people (meaning, in this instance, workers in the productive works) to become members of the local stores', said Mitchell in 1892. But he did admit to the Royal Commission that, while he thought that there were some work people on the committees of individual productive works and certainly some on the committees of retail Societies, there were no work people from any of the Productive works on the Committee of the CWS.

However imperfect the system of production in which, as Mitchell saw it, 'the Wholesale occupied the highest ground', it was a whole by which independent producer co-operatives, and even productive units attached to local Societies, could be judged as second best parts. They needed replacing by CWS units which would feed directly into the single system. Size was put to him as a problem: the CWS was big. Mitchell was unafraid: they were not yet, he would point out, as big as Government itself and Government seemed to manage. (126) Decisions which seemed pragmatic to his detractors, involved him in what he saw as 'great constitutional principles'. When he wanted to refuse the entry of the Co-operative Sundries Manufacturing Society into the CWS in 1891, Neale taunted him, 'why be afraid of 2 or 3 pills?' (127) The C.S.M.S. wanted to manufacture and to supply from other manufacturers, groceries, drugs, patent medicines, etc. Some of its 120 articles would be encroaching on existing CWS production. Allies and friends in business were involved, but Mitchell was adamant. He reached for John Bunyan to say that one small leak might sink a ship, one sin would keep a sinner out of heaven. They were in a 'representative institution'. This was utterly incompatible with the admission of any 'private interests'. 'If a person comes here in the capacity of a representative, and he is a private shareholder in some other society, then you have a private interest conflicting with a representative interest'. It was in these settings that he looked most pig-headed to people who disagreed with him. (128)

Within the single system, production was important to Mitchell, in a way which the familiar label 'consumers co-operation' has served to conceal. He put it an unfamiliar way round, ' we are striving that this wealth which is made in distribution shall belong to those who produce'. (129) 'Co-operation was the one true redemption for the social evils of human life, because it declared that the profits made by every kind of industry belonged to the people who made them (Applause)'. (130) He was stung into putting it together in a single speech when Thomas Hughes criticised the CWS in the inaugural address of the 1887 Congress. (131) Mitchell mounted a hugely ambitious defence of his system. He wanted the Wholesale to start works in every town where they would pay. He wanted them to make everything their members wore. He wanted co-operation to be 'permanently successful'. 'He advised co-operators never to be satisfied until they got control of the entire producing, banking, shipping and every other, interest in the country'. The whole was brought into play when seemingly-trivial parts were being talked about. When considering the replacement of a tea merchant, with whom they had been dealing for years, in 1878, a paper to the General Committee spoke of how 'we must climb to the climax of a perfect organisation'. (132) In his 1887 speech, Mitchell put it thus:

'To whom does profit and the increment of value belong? We hold that, as it was created by the industrious classes, it belonged to them. Profit was made by the consumption of the people, and the consumers ought to have the profit. *But what was the difference between the people and the industrious classes?* (my emphasis). He advised co-operators not to be satisfied until they got control of the entire producing, banking, shipping and every other interest in the country'.

If the circle could only be completed, forms would be found wherein there would be no difference between 'the people' and 'the industrious classes'. That was the gap Mitchell was trying to close. Tom Mann: 'May I put it this way, that your distributive co-operation is merely preliminary to productive co-operation?'. Mitchell, 'that is so'. Tom Mann, 'then productive co-operation is exactly what you are driving at?' Mitchell, 'exactly'. (133)

'Ours is a complete system in itself bound together by a common bond for the best interests of mankind'. (134) Until completion, in what Percy Redfern called 'the final form of industry', internal class conflicts, or as Mitchell called them 'special interests', would have space to grow within the Movement, as they did outside. 'In co-operation there were no class interests'. (135) This was the case against bonus-to-labour, profit-sharing and the like. Mitchell told the Royal Commission that they 'will only tend in the direction of creating a new order of capitalists'. Distributing profits amongst a select few would create a working class aristocracy'. (136) At a meeting at Congress in 1894, he argued with his opponents:

> 'Co-operation ought to be based on the principle of united interest with the societies, and not individuals. Some persons taught that the individual should be the basis... It was not a sound principle to appropriate profit to specially selected persons, on the basis of class interests; such a plan was opposed to the genius of genuine co-operative thought and action which had characterised the Movement since its commencement'. (137)

If profits derived from the work place, they would be sectional. The whole community, the entire body politic should share in any surplus derived from production. It would be better for everyone to have a bit than for some, for instance those nearest to the flour mill or those who worked in it, to have a lot. To Mitchell, personal wealth was not particularly desirable anyway: he disliked it with an old-fashioned plebeian radical temper. (138) It was important for everyone to be comfortable. It was important, too, to have a system in place whose dynamic worked in the right direction, rather than one which might have temporary advantages (say for those living in Leeds, or on top of a coal mine, or for those who married the miller's daughter) but which would have to be revolutionised all over again once wealth had accumulated in a particular channel. Mitchell's project was to find the single (for him necessarily federal) form which was also the universal one. He was not to be satisfied with anything less.

There was much ceremony at the opening of the Wholesale Society's Flour Mill at Dunston-on-Tyne in April 1891: processions, meals and music. As always, there were speeches. At the end of the day Mitchell got up to make a final, seemingly spontaneous speech, which included direct heckling by Edward Vansittart Neale. Mitchell was in an ebullient mood, deep into the romance of statistics. He calculated that the industries in federation with the Wholesale had, to that date, made a profit of £70,000, allowing for interest, depreciation and losses. They employed about 2,000 workers in their productive works. 'Now he asked them whether it was more in the interests of working men that that £70,000 should be divided amongst 70,000 people rather than 2,000 people? (Mr. Neale: "No"). He said yes, and it was more in the interests of mankind (Cheers). They had made capitalists enough in the past. They wanted to make capitalists universal. 'He then explained that in one of the CWS industries it took about £50 to employ a man, in another £87, another £114, another £372, and so on. In the Flour Mills, it would take nearly £1,500 of capital for every man that could be employed. In two corn mills where 200 workers were employed, last year they had made a profit of £40,000:

> 'He asked them would it be in accordance with common sense that 200 people should take £40,000? That was not co-operation. It was diametrically opposed to the spirit and genius of co-operation, that they should divide the profits of working men amongst a few people. He thanked them very cordially, and he should not have made those remarks but for the feeling that they were bound to know both sides of the question, in order that they might understand what it meant'. (139)

It is generally forgotten that the voices arguing for co-partnership during the late nineteenth and early twentieth centuries included arch enemies of the Co-operative Movement like W.H. Lever: and that there was theoretical, principled, working class voices arguing strongly against it. (140)

iv. *Politics, and associational practice.*

Mitchell's politics related to mainstream Party Politics, but were not primarily about them. He once suggested that the Conservatives had done as much for Co-operation as the Liberals.

He ran for office as a Radical Liberal in local election campaigns in Rochdale in 1893 and 1894. This was at a time in the town when old-style Liberalism was being attacked by a growing Independent Labour presence and when alliances between the I.L.P. and Radicals were being pushed. On the Radical side, State Socialism was seen as an obstacle to alliance. (141) At his adoption meeting in 1893 Mitchell was recommended as an 'excellent representative of both labour and capital (Laughter and Applause)'. There were obvious advantages, seen as such by the local Liberal press, in running such a candidate at such a time. "Mr. Mitchell is not exactly a wage earner just now... but he is in the truest sense a man of the people'. (142) He was narrowly defeated by the Conservatives, and again in 1894, having stated 'what he most desired' as 'the working man exercising control over the forces of the nation'. (143) After the second defeat, the *Rochdale Observer* praised him thus: 'He is not a good electioneer. He offered his services to the ward, but that was all; he would not flatter his friends, he would not canvass the indifferent, he would not cajole the unwilling. This is admirable, but it is not electioneering.' (144)

Mitchell advocated Co-operative Parliamentary representation rather early, at the Congress of 1877. He returned to the theme at Lincoln in 1891. In part, he saw the Movement as an interest among other interests, needing seats near to the centre of power in order 'to influence the government of the day in favour of co-operative legislation'. (145) But it was more than that, locally and nationally. It was about control: bringing co-operation into politics rather than politics into co-operation. (146) As with trading, Mitchell was not satisfied with half measures. When the Mayor of Lincoln came to open an exhibition of Co-operative products at the 1891 Congress, Mitchell presented him with the CWS *Annual*. He then took the opportunity to remind him that there were 6,000 members of Lincoln Co-operative Society. Ever ready with statistics, Mitchell said that they contributed £700 a year towards the Corporation. The Mayor was obviously embarrassed. He said he was impartial, and would open exhibitions for private trades people, if asked. Mitchell finished his speech by declaring that 'Co-operators should strive to get the government of the towns they represented more under their own control'. (147)

The language of Mitchell's politics was in an early nineteenth century, and older, plebeian radical tradition. They were 'engaged in an enterprise which had a great future', he told a meeting at the Huddersfield Congress in May 1888, 'embodying government based on the universal voice of the people'. 'The people' was a favourite phrase of his, 'the people of England': 'what we wanted was that capital and its profits should belong to the people, it was through co-operation that this would be accomplished, and when that day dawned it would be a bright and glorious one for the people of England (Applause)'. They were to work for 'the time... not far distant when the vast co-operative body would have some control over the social and political policy of the nation (Applause)'. (148) One of their entitlements to control was, he said in 1882, that 'they contributed largely to the taxes of the nation and as a body they had no voice in the expenditure of those taxes'. (149) His interest in the National Debt was also in this tradition, as was his concern that the people, not diplomatists, should make treaties. Now that 'the principle of reconcilement of interests' was in motion in their Movement, it 'would leave little work for armies and navies as it came to be applied in the future to the greatest of human affairs'. (150)

It was the details of associational form which mattered, and the relationship between detail and democratic principle. Preoccupation with small sums of money, as a way of curbing the audacity of elected persons, has already been considered within the CWS. In 1874 there was a debate within the Movement over the mode of appointing the Central Board of the Co-operative Union. Up until then, the Board had been elected by delegates at Congress, with each Society having the same representation. William Nuttall wanted to introduce a block vote scheme, whereby each Society would get an extra delegate for every 500 members. The terms upon which E.O.

Greening opposed this innovation were interesting. He said that it would do away with 'parliamentary government' and introduce a foreign system, 'a kind of democratic ultra-despotism, voting by mandate'. Mitchell, however, backed the idea, which was not in the end carried. It was 'what the radicals of this country had fought for for the last century - namely equal electoral districts and power concentrated in localities'. (151)

Mitchell's ultimate vision was original, if not entirely thought out. This was teased out of him by Professor Marshall and Tom Mann in front of the Royal Commission on Labour. Space, he conceded (to Tom Mann) should be allowed for municipalities to do whatever it could be shown that they did best. Mitchell was not dogmatically against <u>any</u> state activity. He had, after all, been Secretary to the government-financed Science and Art Classes for many years in Rochdale. 'It would all depend on the circumstances of the case.' But he was concerned in ways which paralleled his doubts about independent producer co-ops. He was concerned about area, or location, and incipient, new inequalities. In October 1892, Tom Mann pressed him to support local state control where it could be effective as an agent of democratic control over production. Mitchell was wary:

> 'If I understand your question aright, I should say no, because a corporation controls only a limited area, and a wider area would be contributed to the advantage of a limited area in the case you put. Our principle is *the widest area possible for the distribution of advantages,* (my emphasis) and if the question were put to me on the basis of the corporations of the

> land where joining together for the combinations of their productions, it would be more in accordance with our line of action. But if one corporation is to engage in production, and receive within that corporation a special benefit to which it might be a hundred other corporations were to contribute to its advantage, I should not altogether adhere to that at once, whatever we might ultimately agree to. (152)

As far as most industry was concerned, every person was to be a Co-operator, affiliated through their local Societies to the aggregate Society, the C.W.S. Every person would have the power to vote for the Committee of the C.W.S. When he was asked by the Commissioners to generalise off the cuff, he proposed that in the co-operative society of the future it would be a matter of more or less direct election of a national, industrial, general committee of management. Marshall was sceptical. 'The result', he felt, 'would be simply a new form of management of certain industries by a Government for the people'. He kept on suggesting that in Mitchell's scheme, citizens would have no more control over industry than they currently did over the national situation which was less familiar to them than Quarterly Meetings in Manchester. At one moment there was an exchange with Gerald Balfour which provides us with a unique glimpse of the less-than-optimistic side of Mitchell. It is somehow reassuring to discover that such a side was there.

> *Balfour.* 'You contemplate the time when everybody in the country will be a member of your co-operative store?'

> *Mitchell.* 'I should like to do so, and I hope I may. I cannot say that my faith is over strong because of the selfishness of mankind, but I do contemplate that such a thing may be brought about by the universal distribution of knowledge of the highest kind'.

The last phrase has an Owenite ring to it. But Mitchell pressed on with practicalities. He was not entirely clear about how direct or effective elections already were within the CWS. Much was left to the autonomy of Societies. But he implied that within his federation there would be, and was already, a greater degree of direct control than currently existed in the dominant arrangements of conventional Politics:

> 'As it stands at present the constituencies elect Parliament, Parliament does not even elect the Government, except in one way, by a sort of negative vote, but if the country were called upon directly to elect the Government - every post from the Prime Minister to the most humble positions - then there would be a comparison to ourselves, if that was done'.

During one of his Rochdale campaigns in 1893, he had argued that 'all government should be conducted by elected executives, and, when elected, those executives should be favourable to the principles to which they gave adhesion when first they sought suffrage'. (153) At the Royal Commission he went rather deeper than his dinner:

> 'If the principle were carried out as I would have it carried out, every citizen would feel the influence of this great and powerful system, from the centre to the circumference, and they would feel that they were associated with something better than what is in existence today, and every citizen would be raised and would occupy a higher and nobler position'. (154)

---

1. *Co-operative News*, 23 March 1895, p.297, piece 'By one who knew him'.

2. For an earlier attempt to get at 'the place of the Co-operative Wholesale Society in the proletarian forces of the world' via consideration of J.T.W. Mitchell, see James Haslam, 'Pioneers and Leaders', in *The Wheatsheaf,* May 1923, p.76.

3. For conveniently presented data on the size and growth of the CWS, see Percy Redfern, *The New History of the CWS*, London, Dent/CWS, 1938, 'Statistical Supplement', pp.531-547.

4. The nearest I have come to Mitchell and Socialism named as such by him is in a personal copy of the *Handbook* of the Edinburgh Co-operative Congress, 1888, which has a rare example of Mitchell's handwriting in it. The Handbook is in the possession of the Library and Information Unit of the CWS in Manchester, from whom I have had much help in writing this essay. A propos of a sermon he had heard on Sunday, 13 May 1883, Mitchell noted down the texts, and then 'the socialistic experiment of Jerusalem may have been a failure. But it ought not to discourage us in doing what we can to bring about some plan of (illegible word) among men. Not only must we bear our own burdens but also each other's burdens'. Haslam...1923 wrote that Mitchell 'gave indication of being an evolutionary socialist who might have written some such volume as *Merrie England* if he had had Blatchford's great literary skill'. At Mitchell's funeral, his pastor at Milton Congregational Chapel, the Rev. J. Hirst Hollowell, called the Co-operative Movement 'the most successful of all embodiments of the Socialistic spirit', *Rochdale Observer,* 23 March 1895. The CWS *Annual*, 'put out by the Committee each year' expressed its project thus in 1886: 'In the present Annual it is our main purpose to explain the growth of thought in connection with human progress, the ideas of the philosophers and the struggles of the workers. We make no pretence to

state the minute particulars of all forms of socialistic thought... Our aim more specially is to place in the hands of the reading portion of our working population a sketch that will enable them to apprehend a subject which has perhaps a stronger claim than any other on the serious attention of all classes of our population'.

5. See an address to the Bolton Co-operative Society at the opening of their Reading and Conversation Rooms in 1877, quoted in F.W. Peaples, *History of the Great and Little Bolton Co-operative Society Ltd: showing 50 years' progress, 1859-1909*, Manchester, 1909, pp.103-4.

6. The quotes by Mitchell on Owen are from Mitchell's testimony to the Royal Commission on Labour on 25 October 1893, for which see 'Evidence before R.C. on Labour 1893-4 XXXIX pt. 1, Questions 1-405'; and from Mitchell's speech as President of the Co-op Congress of 1892, as reported in CN, 11 June 1892 p.609. The 1892 Congress speech contained an historical account of co-operation in Britain back to 1792, going on through the first Congresses of 1831-5 of which Mitchell knew the details. At the 1869 Congress, the first of the new series, Owenites like Henry Travis and William Pare harked back to the 1830's. Mitchell, delegate from Rochdale, related to them thus: 'he did not see any insuperable difficulty in the way of realising the better state of co-operative life which had been foreshadowed, provided we began low enough and proceeded by natural growth', quoted in Arnold Bonner, *British Co-operation: the History, Principles and Organisation of the British Co-operative Movement*, Manchester, 1970, p.80 (Ist edit. 1961). That Mitchell's doubts about Owen were well-founded, perhaps needs no arguing nowadays, but for their justification see Owen's reaction to finding 6 or 7 Co-operative Societies trading in different parts of Carlisle in 1836: 'to my surprise, I found there 6 or 7 co-operative societies... doing well, as they think - that is, making some profit by joint stock trading. It is, however, high time to put an end to the notion very prevalent

in the public mind that this is the social system which we contemplate or that will form any part of the arrangement in the New Moral World', quoted in W. Henry Brown, *A Century of London Co-operation* (n.d.) p.19. In 1884, Mitchell showed his friend William Maxwell the actual plan of Owen's proposed 1822 industrial village/colony which was to have been sited near Liverpool. Maxwell later wrote to W. Henry Brown telling him that this plan made a deep impression on him as he was 'at that time considering a scheme I intended to carry out in the Scottish CWS which, two years afterwards, took form at Shieldhall', see W. Henry Brown, *A Century of Liverpool Co-operation* (Liverpool n.d.) pp.32, 37.

One of the lines of descent for Mitchell's Owenism, in the sense that I am proposing it here, was through Dr. John Watts (1818-1887) the slightly paralysed (and therefore unfit for manual work) son of a Coventry ribbon weaver who became an Owenite missionary. Watts spoke at the first of the new series of Congresses which Mitchell attended in 1869. He was also a speaker at the National Association for the Promotion of Social Science on Co-operation, see *Transactions*, 1860 pp.873-4. He wrote a major series of articles to open the *Co-operative News* in 1871 in which he put forward much of what Mitchell later (already?) represented, and in which he theorised Co-operation as a transition to Communism. For Watts' influence, see Percy Redfern, *John T.W. Mitchell, Pioneer of Consumers Co-operation,* Co-operative Union, Manchester, 1923. Watts and Mitchell were still seeing each other in the 1880's, see CWS General Committee, Minutes 8 Feb. 1884, p.581. Watts intervened at the 1873 Congress on behalf of CWS production against people like Ludlow. A good social/intellectual biography of Watts is needed as much as one on Holyoake.

7. *CN*, 20 Oct. 1894, p.1168.

8. Haslam, op.cit. 1923, p.76; Co-operative Congress Report, 1894, p.138.

9. R., 'Candid Friendship', in *The Wheatsheaf*, Feb. 1922, p.20, a piece on Beatrice Webb, referred to how 'J.T.W. Mitchell, whom she still regards as a genius, became her friend'. When Mitchell turned down the prestigious invitation to become a Director of the Manchester Ship Canal in 1895, the *CN*, 16 March 1895, p.277 used the decision to point up the difference between Mitchell's *exclusive* devotion to public causes and the tendency among younger men to ask 'whether this great slow-moving machine of democracy is worth making sacrifices for'. The *News* saw this as a major problem of the times. For this incident see also CWS General Committee Minutes, 1 March 1895 - 21 June 1895. Beatrice Webb, *My Apprenticeship*, London, Longmans, 1926, p.360 n.1.

10. *CN*, 11 Dec. 1880, pp.308.12.

11. *Rochdale Observer*, 3 April 1895.

12. William Maxwell, 'The Late John Thomas Whitehead Mitchell', in CWS *Annual*, 1886, pp.392-414, p.397: this memoir is the most personal piece of writing we have about Mitchell. Maxwell was Mitchell's equivalent within the Scottish CWS, had obviously been inside Mitchell's home, went with him to the U.S.A. in 1884, and wrote as if he had spoken quite intimately with Mitchell. In the Edinburgh Congress Handbook referred to above, Mitchell recorded his purchase that day of work by Crabbe, Burns and Shakespeare. He would quote from Bunyan, see *CN*, 21 March 1891, pp.268.72.

13. Funeral and Memorial Services for Mr. J.T.W. Mitchell, Milton Chapel, March 20th and 31st 1895, *Addresses by Rev. J. Hirst Hollowell* (Rochdale, 1895), in Rochdale local history collection; *Rochdale Observer*, 23 March 1895; *Co-operative News*, 23 March 1895.

14. *CN*, 27 March 1895, p.297, an appreciation 'By one who knew him'.

15. Maxwell, Memoir, 1896. They had met in temperance, political and Co-op work in Rochdale. The friendship grew closer when Howard's wife and Mitchell's mother died in the same year, 1855. They lived together for a while. Howard remarried, and then in 1861 moved to Liverpool to a new job. Until the end of his life, Mitchell kept a room in John Street, Rochdale for Howard to visit, better furnished than his own.

16. The story of this relationship comes from Maxwell, Memoir, pp.401-2; and from Redfern, Mitchell, 1923, p.32.

17. *Rochdale Observer*, 23 March 1895.

18. Maxwell, Memoir, 1896, p.400.

19. *Rochdale Observer*, 20 March 1895.

20. Beatrice Webb, *My Apprenticeship*, p.359 n.1. Beatrice was quoting, but from whom?

21. *Handbook* of Co-operative Congress, Rochdale 1892, p.154.

22. Prospero, *Mitchell the Leader*, The People's Papers no.4 1928, p.6.

23. Maxwell, Memoir, p.394; *Rochdale Observer*, 20 March 1895.

24. Maxwell, Memoir, p.395.

25. Redfern, Mitchell, 1923, p.49. At the time of his Presidency of the Rochdale Congress in 1892, the piece on him in the *Rochdale Observer* saw the L. and P.Y.S. liquidatorship as 'the only flaw in the ointment of Mr. Mitchell's relations with the Pioneers, and when he can give them a good

report, as all hope he soon may, they will be perfectly satisfied with him', R.O., 4 June 1892.

26. The convention was set by Sidney Pollard, 'Nineteenth-century Co-operation: from Community Building to Shopkeeping', in Asa Briggs and John Saville eds., *Essays in Labour History*, London, Macmillan, 1960, pp.74-112; but then see Philip N. Backstrom, *Christian Socialism and Co-operation in Victorian England: Edward Vansittart Neale and the Co-operative Movement*, London, Croom Helm, 1974.

27. CWS G.C. Minutes, 22 March 1895 and other entries.

28. T.W. Mercer, *Towards the Co-operative Commonwealth*, Manchester, 1936, p.93, 'if ever a man incarnated the spirit of an institution, John Mitchell did'.

29. *CN*, 30 April 1892: 'Now for the first day's President we are to have Mr. Mitchell the "spouse" of the Wholesale, and was there ever a more loving husband or a father that ever looked after his progeny better?', quoted in H.B. Wilkinson, *Old Hanging Ditch* London and Manchester, 1910, p.228; see also Maxwell, *Memoir*, 'someone has said that the Wholesale Society was his spouse and their members his family'; see also *CN*, 23 March 1895, 'Friendships he has sacrificed, rather than sacrifice, in his estimation, the Wholesale and its interests. He cared for it - for he was a father in this respect at least - just as the parent cares for his child...'.

30. Funeral and Memorial Services for Mr. J.T.W. Mitchell... 1895.

31. George Jacob Holyoake theorised association more deliberately than anyone else near to Mitchell; see Peter Gurney, 'George Jacob Holyoake: Socialism, Association and Co-operation in nineteenth century England', in S. Yeo ed. *New*

Views of Co-operation, London, Routledge, 1988. In *Organisation: Not of Arms but of Ideas*, London, J. Watson, 1853, Holyoake also used the marriage metaphor, but not in a reductive way: 'Let him who takes an associate, at the same time understand that he takes a master. It is equally true of marriage, of friendship, as of confederation. Companionship implies the intention of mutual service, service includes mutual submission... Organisation is a vow; it involves a plan of life.' Elsewhere Holyoake suggested that 'Association is a moral art As well as a new form of economy'. I owe these references to Peter Gurney, whose forthcoming thesis has a chapter on Holyoake.

32. CWS General Committee Minutes, 2 May 1884 onwards.

33. I am taking some of my information here from a hostile source, H.B. Wilkinson, *Old Hanging Ditch*, London and Manchester, 1910 to which the late Roy Garrett of the Co-operative Union kindly drew my attention.

34. General Committee Minutes, 23 May 1884, p.206.

35. *CN*, 23 March 1895, piece 'By one who knew him'.

36. *CN*, 13 Sept. 1879, p.596..

37. For the Leman Street story, see CN, 13 Sept. 1879, pp.595-7; for the Pitman incident, see CN, 12 March 1881, pp.161-6.

38. *CN*, 14 June 1884, pp.553-4.

39. G.C. Minutes, 20 Dec. 1884.

40. G.C. Minutes, 29 Dec. 1884.

41. For attendance at General and sub-Committee meetings: 7/6d. per meeting and 3/9d. extra if a second meeting was

attended on the same day. Conferences: 5/-, and for overnight stay, an extra 7/-. It was also resolved 'that the Chairman be not paid but honorary'. In future, quarterly balance sheets issued by the Society, amounts received by each Director for railway fares and other expenses were to be inserted.

42. *CN*, 11 June 1892.

43. The same 1892 Presidential speech, but I have taken this bit from H.B. Wilkinson, *Old Hanging Ditch*, London and Manchester, 1910, p.231.

44. *CN*, 13 Dec. 1879, p.805.

45. For Crabtree, see *Dictionary of Labour Biography*, vol.1, pp.88-9. This volume, together with some entries in vol.2, is the best 'secondary' work on the history of the Co-operative Movement to have appeared since G.D.H. Cole.

46. *CN*, 10 Sept. 1881, pp.601-5.

47. The same, p.614.

48. See a speech in Dundee on 17 Sept. 1881, in *CN*, 1 Oct. 1881, p.659.

49. The piece was called 'Caesarism and Federation', and is quoted at length in Philip N. Backstrom, *Christian Socialism and Co-operation in Victorian England: Edward Vansittart Neale and the Co-operative Movement*, London, Croom Helm, 1974, p.113.

50. *CN*, 9 Sept. 1882, p.616. The issues were substantial. They included a CWS grant to the Amalgamated Society of Railway Servants, see *CN*, 9 Sept. 1882, p.606 and Mitchell's views on the CWS Committee's powers over employees, concerning a strike at the Heckmondwike Shoe Works.

51. *Rochdale Observer*, 27 March 1895, p.2.

52. Mitchell later spoke from this experience on a number of occasions. At the Quarterly Meeting of the CWS Newcastle Branch (*CN*, 8 Sept. 1883) he used the L and Y.P.S., story to emphasise his case that Co-operative production could only be successful if the Societies were loyal and bought the goods. In other words, selling outside the Movement was, in this case and for Mitchell, necessary not desirable. At the Lincoln Congress he said: 'he was a firm believer in Co-operative production in which the Wholesale occupied the highest ground. As the liquidator of a productive society, he knew the difficulty of disposing of goods'.

53. Maxwell, Memoir, p.405.

54. *CN*, 9 June 1883, pp.511-19.

55. *CN*, 8 March 1884, pp.187-191.

56. *CN*, 8 Sept. 1883, pp.795-7, 802-3.

57. Backstrom, *Christian Socialism...*, p.213.

58. *CN*, 23 March 1895, p.297.

59. Ben Jones, *Co-operative Production*, Oxford, O.U.P., 1894, p.111, quoting from a Report of the Society for Promoting Working Men's Association.

60. *Transactions of the National Association for the Promotion of Social Science*, 1873, p.516. I owe this reference to Peter Gurney's thesis.

61. Congress, Oxford, 1882, p.3. I owe this reference to Peter Gurney's thesis.

62. Throughout most of Mitchell's life, Congress tended to be under the aegis of the Christian Socialists, the *Co-operative News* more susceptible to the CWS position. But each are invaluable sources for the other positions.

63. Backstrom, *Christian Socialism*, p.211, quoting from the Holyoake papers.

64. Beatrice Webb, *My Apprenticeship*, London, Longmans, 1926, Diary entry for 28 March 1889.

65. The same, Diary entry for June 1889.

66. In *The Economist* in 1821 Philadelphus, a middle-class Owenite, defended the practices of the Co-operative and Economical Society of London against 'men (who)... have already endeavoured to ridicule our idea of mending the world by such carnal means as beef and pudding'. 'We shall see', he added. He was attacking reformers who saw the answer as Political, in this instance, suffrage reform, together with those who advocated at a stroke revolution, concentrating on men's hearts and minds rather than on material, associational forms. Against such views Philadelphus set permanent association, through which the common people could 'unite heart and hand for the acquisition of those things, the value of which is palpable to the senses, namely the good things of this life'. As he saw it, no authority had the right to prevent the common people associating in this way, and furthermore 'it is entirely within their power'. It was an available form. In a debate between a Pemberton Co-operator (William Carson) and John Doherty in July 1830, Doherty had a go at Co-operative trading:

> 'when he heard men talk about getting profit from every mouthful they eat, he confessed his opinion was somewhat

> changed. According to this doctrine, all they had to do was to sit down and eat all before them in order to become completely happy (laughter). The more they eat the richer they would become'.

For Philadelphus's views, see *The Economist*, 27 Oct. 1821; for his identity, see *Bulletin of the Society for the Study of Labour History*, no.43, p.14, a piece by Gregory Claeys. For the Carson-Doherty debate, see Robin Thornes, 'The early development of the Co-operative Movement in W. Yorkshire, 1827-1863', unpublished D.Phil thesis, University of Sussex, 1984.

67. *CN*, 27 April 1878, p.264; 4 May 1878, p.281.

68. A tribute from an artist - Miss Nora Batson - who had been commissioned to do a portrait of Mitchell for the CWS, see *CN*, 23 March 1895, p.296.

69. Maxwell, Memoir... CWS *Annual*, 1896.

70. Hirst Hollowell in his funeral address, quoted above.

71. His friend Abraham Howard, quoted by Hirst Hollowell, and in the Maxwell, Memoir, p.413.

72. *Handbook*, of Co-operative Congress, Rochdale 1892, piece written by William Robertson, a reporter on the *Rochdale Observer.*

73. Halstead was later secretary to the Co-operative Productive Federation, his reminiscences are in *The Co-operative Official*, vol.III, no.31, Oct. 1922, p.179.

74. Cutting from the *Daily Chronicle*, in a press cuttings

volume in the Manchester Central Reference Library, Manchester Newspaper Cuttings, 1889-1896, vol.3, F.942, 7889.M119, p.127. For another eye witness at a Quarterly, see the London correspondence of the *Bradford Observer* at the Feb. 14th 1891 meeting, quoted in CN, 28 March 1891, p.305; and see also *Rochdale Observer*, 20 March 1895.

75. Maxwell, Memoir, p.407.

76. Mr. Shillito, Vice-Chairman of the CWS in his graveside address.

77. Robert Holt, President of the Rochdale Equitable Pioneers, in the *Rochdale Observer*, 3 April 1895, at the first meeting of the R.E.P. following Mitchell's death.

78. Haslam, 1923 piece cited above.

79. For this terminology, see Stephen Yeo, 'Three Socialisms: Statism, Collectivism, Associationism', in William Outhwaite and Mike Mulkay eds, *Social Theory and Social Criticism*, Oxford, Blackwells, 1987; and 'Notes on Three Socialisms, mainly in late nineteenth and early twentieth century Britain', in Carl Levy ed. *Socialism and the Intelligentsia*, London, Routledge, 1987; and 'Socialism, the State and some oppositional Englishness', in Robert Colls and Phillip Dodd eds., *The Idea of Englishness: Politics and Culture, 1880-1920*, London, Croom Helm, 1986.

80. Sidney and Beatrice continued to study Co-operation throughout their lives, in separate treatments of the Movement in Britain as well as in their works on *Industrial Democracy, A Socialist Constitution, Soviet Communism*, etc. D.C. Jones has focussed on their analysis of producer co-operation in a critical way in 'The Economics of British Producer Co-operatives', unpublished D.Phil thesis, University of Cornell, 1974, pp.3-48, 57-9, 74, 277-9, 292, 342-5; see also his 'British Economic

Thought on Association of Labourers 1848-1974', in *Annals of Public and Co-operative Economy*, vol.47, no.I, Jan-March 1976 and 'British Producer Co-operatives and the Views of the Webbs on Participation and Ability to Survive', in *Annals...*, 1, 1975.

81. *My Apprenticeship*, Chap.VII, section on 'The Co-operative Movement'. This section needs reading in its entirety for the beautifully expressed ambivalence of Beatrice, as well as for her novelist's eye trained on well known figures in and around the Co-op Movement during the late 1880's-early 1890's.

82. Quoted in 'Notes on *The Co-operator*', in T.W. Mercer, *Co-operation's Prophet: The Life and Letters of Dr. William King of Brighton, with a reprint of The Co-operator, 1828-1830*, Manchester, Co-operative Union, 1947, p.183.

83. CN, 23 May 1891, p.495.

84. CN, 20 Oct. 1894, p.1168.

85. Redfern, Mitchell, 1923, p.43.

86. James Haslam, *Accrington and Church Industrial Co-operative Society Limited, History of 50 years progress, 1860-1910*, Manchester, 1910, pp.61-3, also reported in CN, 14 Nov. 1874.

87. Royal Commission on Labour... Q.153.

88. Co-operative Congress, Newcastle, 1880, meeting at Gateshead Town Hall, 17 May 1880.

89. Speech at Conference of Co-operators in the Northern Section of the Central Board, in the Mechanics Institute, Chester-le-Street, in CN, 3 Aug. 1878, pp.500-03.

90. *Handbook*, Co-op Congress, Rochdale 1892, p.154.

91. R.E.P.S. General Committee, Minutes, 5 Jan. 1857.

92. I am taking this from Prospero, *Mitchell, The Leader,* p.7; there is also a sympathetic account of the controversy about what was then called 'bounty to labour', in Benjamin Jones, *Co-operative Production*, 1894, pp.260-65.

93. The controversy broke through into G.J. Holyoake's paper *The Counsellor* in 1861. This was the paper which lasted for a brief time, between the demise of *The Reasoner* and the start of *The Secular World*. It is on open shelves in the basement of the Bishopsgate Institute Library, now a major repository for Co-op material which can be studied while listening, through the lift shaft, to symphony orchestras practising upstairs. *The Counsellor* asked William Cooper, financial clerk of the R.E.P.S., to do a survey among religious denominations in Rochdale on the bonus-to-labour question. The results were reported in Sept. 1861, p.7. *The Counsellor* stirred it up by advising Co-operators to keep away from the Hard Shells as the Independents, they said, were called in Lancashire and the Gutta Perchaists, as the Wesleyans were known, 'until the principle of the participation of profits is established'. Abraham Howard, President of the R.E.P.S., then had to rebuke Cooper for being party to bringing religious differences into Co-operation, Nov. 1861, p.18. In the R.E.P.S. Minute Book, the moving letter of rebuke by Howard is written out in full. It is one of those bits of handwriting which has the power to get one right back into the moment it came from. I was led into this controversy by the *D.L.B.* vol.1 entry on William Cooper, 1822-1868.

94. *Rochdale Observer*, 4 June 1892.

95. *CN*, 20 Oct. 1894, p.1168. 'That we do not allow any of our rooms at Leicester Shoe Works for the use of dancing as requested by the employees of the works', was a resolution recorded in the CWS General Committee Minutes, 5 Dec. 1884,

p.13. But I do not know enough of the background to be able to read this properly.

96. It was at the opening of the Flour Mills at Dunston, *CN*, 25 April 1891, p.390 'They said that they had gone on their own footing for many years past, and that they intended to remain "a peculiar people, zealous of good works" (Loud cheers)'.

97. Opening an exhibition at Tynemouth, see *CN*, 20 Aug. 1892, p.920.

98. There was a nice example of this when a deputation of the Labour Association came to Manchester in 1885 to press 'true co-operative principles' on the CWS, see *CN*, 10 Oct. 1885, p.935. Mitchell's smile on this occasion, if I am not mistaken, had an edge to it. He listened to the arguments of Neale, Greening and co., said that they might differ over methods but not goals, offered to print what they had said, and finally said that they in the CWS were glad to have had that interview 'because they had been able to gather the views and sentiments of those with whom they did not come into frequent contact'. See also Mitchell's tribute to Edward Vansittart Neale at the Dewsbury Congress of 1888, in *CN*, 26 May 1888, p.492, a year in which Neale was President of Congress. At a time when dispute between the two sides was at its height Mitchell said: 'They might have differences of opinion as to means to an end, but he trusted their end was the same, (hear hear). They might travel on different roads, but he trusted that when these roads were gone over they might accomplish the work they desired, and that work was that the industrious class of this and every other country should at last find that what is called profit and increment of value shall find their way into the pockets of the industrious classes. (Hear hear and Applause) That was what their friend Mr. Neale had worked for, and he trusted that what Mr. Neale desired might be accomplished, though they might not always walk on the same road'.

Ben Jones made eclecticism into a class principle in an interesting way which contrasts strongly with the opponents of the CWS among the Christian Socialists of whom, incidentally, Neale was the most open to the different-routes-but-same-destination view put by Mitchell above. Mitchell was also capable of being harshly exclusive.

99. Samuel Smiles, *Self Help* (1859) 1958 edit. with an introduction by Asa Briggs, p.284.

100. A phrase of the Rochdale Pioneers of 1844, in a statement of their 'objects and plans'.

101. General Booth, *In Darkest England and the Way Out*, London, Salvation Army, 1890, p.142. In the Appendix pp.xxiii-iv of this book (which was ghosted by W.T. Stead) there was an account of 'The Co-operative Experiment at Ralahine'.

102. Many thanks to Pete Gurney for this reference on management, from his thesis draft (1987). I was led back to *In Darkest England* by it, to find the E.T. Craig lineage.

103. *CN*, 25 April 1891, p.389.

104. Listed in Redfern, Mitchell, 1923, pp.69-70.

105. In a volume of newspaper cuttings, 1888-96, in Manchester Central Reference Library, vol.3, F942, 7889, M.119, p.127.

106. Co-operative Congress, Glasgow 1876, p.5.

107. Percy Redfern, John T.W. Mitchell, *Pioneer of Consumers Co-operation*, Manchester, Cooperative e Union, 1923, p.35.

108. 4 June 1892.

109. Royal Commission on Labour, Mitchell's evidence.

110. Co-operative Congress, Carlisle, 1887, p.7.

111. Cooperative Congress, Bristol, 1893, p.132.

112. CN, 7 April 1877, p.16.

113. Meeting at the Co-operative Congress, Huddersfield, 19 May 1888, p.10. For this notion of a common bond used in a moving argument against religious and political differences within Co-operation, see Rochdale E.P.S. General Committee Minutes for Quarterly Meeting on 6 Jan 1862, letter by Abraham Howard rebuking William Cooper and others over *The Counsellor* row, 'the present Co-operative Movement does not intend to meddle with the various religious or political differences which now exist in society but by a common bond namely that of self-interest to join together the means, the energies and talents of all for the common benefit of each'.

114. Thos. Tweddell, 'Two reasons why Co-operation succeeds', in *The Wheatsheaf*, vol.II, no.8 Feb. 1898, p.114.

115. 'Complete Co-operation', pp.186-202 of *Co-operative Life*, London, 1889, a reprint of a series of lectures given in the Workings Men's College, London. The anecdote is on p.192.

116. *CN*, 16 March 1912, p.327.

117. Productive Committee Minutes, 14 March 1895. A new-broom manager at Crumpsall was trying to sort out more lax methods which seemed to be associated with Hayes. Two visitors from the PC had gone to Crumpsall to sort out some aggravation. 'Messrs. Hayes and Procter in the first place stated that Mr. Marshall did not understand co-operative ways, by which they appeared to mean that co-operative employees should have a certain amount of laxity allowed them, such as

coming a few minutes later in the morning etc., to what they would have in working for a private firm'. Marshall was concerned to increase productivity and cut down on overtime. He said that in the handmade biscuit department, 'with half the hands he could turn out the same amount of work'. On March 21st Hayes and Marshall had to attend the PC. A reconciliation was attempted, 'it was understood that Mr. Hayes and Mr. Marshall would consult together and that Mr. Hayes would carry out any suggestions which were made of a practicable character and which would be an improvement'.

118. See *CN*, 14 Sept. 1889, pp.982-991.

119. *CN*, 12 March 1887, p.246.

120. I have taken the story of this strike from the *Co-operative News* and the CWS General Committee Minutes. It can be followed in more detail in Ben Jones, *Co-operative Production* and in Backstrom, *Christian Socialism.* It would be worth researching in more detail as part of wider work on CWS production, perhaps starting with all the labour disputes referred to in Ben Jones.

121. Percy Redfern, 'The Mitchell Centenary and its significance', in *The Peoples Year Book,* 1929, pp.15-16.

122. *CN*, 23 Oct. 1880, p.697.

123. *CN*, 8 March 1884, P.79.

124. The entire correspondence was copied in long hand into the R.E.P.S. General Committee Minute Books, see Committee Meeting, 21st April 1881, in a way which, as with the Abraham Howard letter in *The Counsellor* case above, gives one a marvellous feeling of direct contact with the people involved.

125. Co-operative Congress, Lincoln, 1891, p.104.

126. *CN*, 3 Aug. 1878, pp.500-03, speech at a Conference of Co-operators in the Northern Section of the Central Board.

127. *CN*, 21 March 1891, pp.268-272.

128. See, for instance, his opposition to the CWS giving a donation to the National Co-operative Festival in 1893, on the grounds that this was an event promoted by the Agricultural and Horticultural Association and a few private individuals, not authorised by the Movement, in *CN*, 17 June 1893, Quarterly Meeting, pp.646-652; and for his opposition to production by large retail societies more or less in opposition to the general federation, see Percy Redfern, Mitchell, 1923 pp.52 and following. The unsorted Greening papers in the Co-operative Union Library would be valuable sources for these episodes.

129. Royal Commission on Labour... Q.150. Years later, in his *Mitchell, The Leader*, 'Prospero' commented, 'the new idea of abolishing profit and all special interests in profit, by using the CWS as the means of the whole body of consumers producing for themselves, was not grasped'. Similarly, Percy Redfern wrote in 1928, that:

> 'if the consumers' theory is not felt to be radical and challenging, it is simply because so few of us have yet taken it seriously, and so fail to see where it is pointing'.

'John T.W. Mitchell, A Centenary Appreciation', in *The Co-operative Review*, II, 1928, pp.176-180.

130. *CN*, 13 Sept. 1884, p.834.

131. Co-operative Congress, Carlisle 1887, p.7.

132. CWS General Committee Minutes, volume covering 29 June 1878-4 Sept. 1880.

133. Royal Commission on Labour... Q.372-3.

134. The same... Q.293.

135. *CN*, 13 Sept. 1884, p.832. Mitchell was launching a lifeboat at Tynemouth, called "Co-operator, 1".

136. *CN*, 13 June 1891, pp.609-10; and *CN*, 19 May 1894, p.530: 'He did not want a section of co-operators to be elevated at the expense of the rest, that would be creating a privileged and wealthy aristocratic class. Profits should go to the entire body politic'.

137. The 1894 speech was at a meeting at Congress (see Co-operative Congress, 1894, p.138) celebrating the Jubilee of 1844. I owe this reference to Gill Scott.

138. See his speech at the 10th Quarterly Conference of Midland Co-operative Societies in Leicester, in *CN*, 16 Jan. 1875 pp.29-30.

139. *CN*, 25 April 1891.

140. In 1912 Lever was to print an address on co-partnership which he had given to none other than E.O. Greening's Agricultural and Horticultural Association. Not surprisingly, his tone was not unlike that of General Booth quoted above.

The Scottish Co-operative Movement, where it was a live issue during the 1890's and early 1900's is the best place to pick up the working class and socialist case against. See *The Scottish Co-operator,* 19 Aug. 1904, p.772; 4 Nov. 1904, p.1245; 18 Nov. 1904, p.1093; 25 Nov. 1904, p.1116; 16 Dec. 1904, p.1192; 6 Jan. 1905, p.20. 'Is it not possible that he (the anti-bonusite) may be pervaded by something nobler than greed?', asked one correspondent who expounded a long case against 'making a favoured class inside the Co-operative Movement'. 'Is it not possible that he may be pervaded by the spirit of principle?' (*SC*, 19 Aug. 1904, p.772). In April 1905 'Democritus' wrote out the case against in a very trenchant letter, see *SC*, 28 April 1905, pp.407-8.

141. See a long letter by Charles Oakeby in the *Rochdale Observer*, 21 Oct. 1893, p.4.

142. *Rochdale Observer*, 4 Nov. 1893, p.4.

143. *R.O.*, 24 Oct. 1894.

144. *R.O.*, 3 Nov. 1894, p.4. For an attack on private shopkeepers by Mitchell during this second campaign, see *Rochdale Times*, 1 Nov. 1894.

145. 'They not only wanted leasehold enfranchisement, they wanted power to compel landlords to let land for co-operative purposes', Co-operative Congress, Lincoln, 1891, p.2.

146. A formulation of William Maxwell's, at the Congress of 1897, see Sydney Elliott, *Sir William Maxwell: A Pioneer of National and International Co-operation*, Manchester, Co-operative Union, 1923.

147. Co-operative Congress, Lincoln, 1891, p.3.

148. Public meeting at Cooperative Congress, Plymouth, 1886, in *CN*, 19 June 1886, p.581.

149. *CN*, 13 April 1882, pp.204-5, speech at the coming-of-age celebrations of he Huddersfield Industrial Co-operative Society.

150. *CN*, 27 Sept. 1884, p.857, and p.860. For Mitchell's internationalism, see Co-operative Congress, Newcastle-on-Tyne, 1880, p.42; and speech of welcome to French Co-operators at the Oldham Congress of 1885; and speech at opening of London CWS building, Leman Street, in *CN*, 12 Nov. 1887, pp.1138-9. Co-op Congress proceedings have always been more international in flavour than the T.U.C.

151. Co-operative Congress, Halifax, 1874, pp.21-2.

152. Royal Commission on Labour... Q.392.

153. *Rochdale Observer*, 4 Nov. 1893, p.6.

154. Royal Commission on Labour... Questions 289, 288.